World War II Cavalcade

An Offer I Couldn't Refuse

World War II Cavalcade

Cavalcade

An Offer I Couldn't Refuse

by
John L.
Munschauer

Sunflower University Press®

P. O. Box 1009 • 1531 Yuma • Manhattan, Kansas 66505-1009 USA

ISBN 0-89745-194-5

Cover: From a painting by H. Charles McBarron,
"Cuidado," on Luzon, Philippine Islands, 1945.
From the "Army in Action Scenes," Department
of the Army.

Edited by Amie Goins
Layout by Lori L. Daniel

Contents

Part One
Scalpel

Part Two
Bayonet

Part Three
Sword

Acknowledgments

ON APRIL 13, 1945, Russell E. McLogan joined Company K of the 63rd Infantry. If I met him at the time I don't remember it. He was one of many youngsters coming into the company in the spring of '45 to fill the void left by casualties. Many of these men, hardly out of high school, were soon shot. McLogan himself got it on June 21, but fortunately survived to return home, have a family, and in retirement write a history of his war experiences. Fortunately for me, we were each doing the same thing. Well, not quite. He is a born researcher, a peruser of archives, an historian; I am a storyteller. Hence the product of our work is quite different, but I like to think complementary.

My stories of the war are as accurate as I can possibly make them, but I do not claim to be an historian. I am trying to relate a human experience, and to me it usually isn't essential to determine whether a particular incident happened in April or May, but if it happened in May, that is when I want to place the story. Thanks to McLogan, I can claim that most historical background is accurate. He has shared his information with me, sent me background on tactical situations, and filled me in on interesting details. Information I presented on the USS *General Langfit*, a Navy troop ship, is accurate because McLogan looked it up in *Troopships of World War II* and sent the information on to me.

Colonel Arndt Mueller, a major and commander of the 3rd Battalion of the 63rd Infantry at the time I joined it, has followed my manuscript and kept me on track. Much of the information he sent me was so interesting I decided to include it in my book.

I have consulted the National Archives and they have been helpful. *The 6th Infantry Division in World War II, 1939-1945*, published in May 1947 by the Infantry Journal Press (Washington, D.C.), was a good source of information.

Introduction

*A*S A CHILD I saw *Cavalcade*, a film that chronicled the life of an English family at the turn of the century. It was about war and it was about peace. It was about joy and about sorrow. A parade of events made the film interesting; what the people caught up in the parade did about it made it engrossing.

Why I remembered this long-forgotten film is a mystery, except that I had been writing about World War II when *Cavalcade* came to mind to give me a formula for handling my material. I began marching in a cavalcade when one of Roosevelt's earliest drafts dragged me into the prewar Army of Jones' *From Here to Eternity*. It was thoroughly corrupt; it was thoroughly fascinating. I have to tell about it. The Army turned me into a surrogate surgeon. I saw great medicine; I saw malpractice. I practiced medicine. I can take out your appendix; unfortunately I can't remember how to stitch you back together. Stories from *"M*A*S*H"* were not new to me. But my medical career almost ended when I was put in a mental hospital. I have to tell about it.

While I was dragged into the Army kicking and screaming, I did an about-face and grabbed a flag to help lead the parade. That almost ended when my Infantry platoon decided to kill me. I have to tell about it.

When the war was over and I was on duty in Korea, a Japanese army unit presented me with a regimental sword, and Japanese civilians held a banquet in my honor, got me drunk, and sent me off with a geisha. I have to tell about it.

Cavalcade suggests a march — the past moving forward to the present and on into future. The greatest event of the century, World War II, created forces that are propelling us forward into the 21st century: in technology, at a pace that seems to increase as the years go by; in human affairs, where there has been progress. Sometimes the war seems to have left us with a mindset that has led us in the wrong direction at times — more astray than you can possibly imagine, judging from the stories my daughter brought home from school, especially stories relating to atrocities by soldiers, and, of course, the dropping of the bomb. I feel I can speak for the soldiers — at least those with whom I served — and present a different picture, but the teacher had another explanation: "Your father didn't know what was going on because he was there." I am still trying to figure that one out, but all I can say is, he didn't know either.

One thing is sure. My generation did plant many seeds that grew and became an important part of the present — most of it good, some of it bad. If, other than to entertain, and to give in to a compulsion to get war stories off my chest, I would like to present as honest a picture as possible of what we were like then, perhaps to help better understand the seeds we planted. If this small snapshot of the life and times helps some historian, I will be pleased. And I would be most pleased if it would help my daughter and her teacher see past events in an historical perspective, rather than interpreting history with today's values.

Certain of the attitudes and language of the times that I reflect in this book may offend some, but I am trying to tell it the way it was. In today's light, some of it doesn't please me. Back then, I called Japanese "Japs," and did it with considerable hatred. I don't hate them now and today would never call them Japs. But I am left with never-ending questions about them. Wary — that's the word that applies to them. And I am not without questions about us. Worry — that's the word that applies to us. Whatever the heritage, there was a time when the country can be proud of what it did, and none more proud than the Infantry. I dedicate this book to them.

My Cavalcade

A CAVALCADE IS a procession, especially a military procession with horses. By my time, horses were pretty much gone in the Army, although I did ride them briefly in an Army ROTC. During the war, I marched in a cavalcade as a foot soldier in one long procession that took me to the following posts in the United States and Asia:

Fort Niagara, New York. April 11, 1941 — Induction.

Fort Bragg, North Carolina. April 1941-February 1942 — 66th General Hospital; training to be a surgical technician.

Fort Dix, New Jersey. February-April 1942 — With

the Harvard Medical Unit known as the 5th General Hospital, awaiting departure overseas.

Fort Niagara, New York. February-September 1942 — Station Hospital as a surgical technician.

Carlisle Barracks, Pennsylvania. September-November 1942 — Medical Field Service School; Officers Candidate School.

Fitzsimmons General Hospital Medical Technicians School, Colorado. November 1942-August 1944 — Company Commander of a training unit.

Fort Benning, Georgia. August-October 1944 — Officers Special Basic Training Unit; Retreading, graduated as an infantry officer.

Fort McClellan, Alabama. October-December 1944 — Assigned to a basic training unit for Nisei (second-generation Japanese Americans).

Fort Ord, California. December 1944 — Infantry training and preparation for overseas assignment.

USS *General Langfit*, January 19-February 18, 1945 — Guest of the Navy on a cruise from San Francisco, with a stop at Hollandia, New Guinea, then on to Tacloban, Leyte, Philippine Islands.

Tramp ship, name unknown. Early March 1945 — Travel to Luzon.

Sixth Infantry Division, Luzon, Philippines and Korea. March 17-December 2, 1945 — Company K, 3rd Battalion, 63rd Infantry; platoon leader.

USS *Golden City* to Tacoma, Washington; train to Fort Knox, Kentucky. December 1945 — Home and job finished.

Part One

Scalpel

Chapter 1

An Offer I Couldn't Refuse

 KNEW THE game Roosevelt was playing; I didn't have to get trapped. But I had buried my head in the sand. Now, I had to face the consequences. On April 11, 1941, at 5:30 in the morning, a jangling alarm announced the dreaded doomsday. I wasn't alone in my misery. In a house on Auburn Avenue, in another on Elm Street, in houses on Genesee and Lathrop Streets, in houses here and there throughout the city of Buffalo, other alarms rang. Men climbed out of bed, staggered to the bathroom, flicked on the lights, rubbed their eyes to adjust to the glare, and stared at the face in the bathroom mirror. On Niagara Street, Murphy, seeing himself, vomited in the sink. Menkovitz, too hung over to stand the glare, flicked off the light. To shave or not to shave, that was the question. For some the answer came back, "Aw shit, why shave?" Kelley was still too drunk to shave.

I shaved, but I couldn't get breakfast down, although that had nothing to do with alcohol. My mother had prepared my favorites: pancakes with real maple syrup, two fried eggs, bacon, and coffee. Don't believe that story about prisoners wanting their favorite meal before an execution. The two fried eggs stared up from the plate looking like the jaundiced eyes of a cadaver. I was headed for the gallows — almost. Roosevelt was screwing around drafting men into the Army as part of his machinations to get us into the war against Hitler. I and hundreds of other guys in Buffalo had opened a letter that said: "Greetings, be at your draft board on April 11 by 7:00 a.m. or else. . . ."

I got the bacon down. Attempts to be cheerful fell flat. My father started reciting his usual litany of Roosevelt's warmongering crimes, but then trailed off. What was the use? Roosevelt had me by the balls. Better to say my farewells and get Dad to drive me to the neighborhood draft board. We tried to say something to each other along the way, but soon gave up. Were this today, an April in the 1990s, we would be expected to hug and slobber about how much we loved each other. I liked the old way. Sometimes emotions come through better in silence. You can hear the lump in the other person's throat.

Dad drove east on Main Street to Minnesota Avenue, turned right, and after a half a block stopped in front of Public School 63, the site for a rendezvous with my draft board. As I was getting out of the car, Dad said, "Goodbye, Lap Robe." My middle name is Lathrop. When I was a little kid, Dad used to give a whistle and say, "Where's Lap Robe?" This was the signal for me to get a book and crawl up on his lap. I'd forgotten about that.

Inside, about 30 of us stood around. A couple of guys who seemed to know each other were talking; most were quiet. I didn't know anybody. I wasn't raised in this neighborhood. We had moved from Auburn Avenue to this section of Buffalo known as Central Park while I was in college. The head of the draft board, an avuncular guy with a Rotary Club pin in his lapel, tried to mingle, be friendly, but we just wanted to get on with whatever we were going to do. So did he. He kept looking at his watch and asking, "Anybody here know John Jones; anybody seen him?" Nobody answered. With that, he made a little speech and loaded us on a bus.

Erie Community College is located in downtown Buffalo in what was once the city's post office. Built in 1910 in the Gothic style complete with spires, flamboyant tracery and carvings, and false gables, it is a glorious old building — a triumph of restoration and urban renewal. Seeing it today, it is hard to imagine how dismal it looked in 1941. Erected in the lower end of Buffalo's Main Street in a commercial area of warehouses, ship chandlers, and freight yards, in a section of the city that soon passed its peak after the turn of the century, it went slowly downhill thereafter, finally succumbing to a knockout punch during the Great Depression of the '30s. By then many of the surrounding buildings had been abandoned to rats. The fine 19th-century hotels, if they survived at all, became flophouses. In the midst of this decay, in a kind of guilt by location, the post office picked up the appearance of yet another rotting structure. Even so, its grandeur might have shown through, except that from coal-fired trains in the nearby freight yards, from ships in the harbor, and from a city heated by coal furnaces, years of soot had settled inches of grime on its every surface, obliterating the beauty beneath. It had become a building you went into, did your business, and got out of — and out of the area, before being accosted by some drunken seaman from one of the flophouses.

We draftees, looking and feeling as dejected as any flophouse drunk, were taken to this dreary building — not to the main entrance that still retained some dignity, but down an alley to its rear where we descended stone steps to the basement where coal bins had been cleared to make room for an Army induction station. Men who had arrived ahead of us from other draft boards were standing around naked, their bare feet on the cold stone floor. With millions of World War II veterans having told too many times the story of their first days in the Army, there is no point in reviving them here, except to repeat some of the dialogue to bring back happy memories for any of those warriors who may still be alive: "Strip. Line up. Grab your pecker, milk it down. Bend over. Pull your cheeks apart. No, stupid. Your ass. Say 'ah.' Hold still. All you're going to feel is a pinprick. Let me see the bottom of your right foot. Your *right*. . . . Nevermind, now the other."

We felt like baboons being picked over by other baboons as medical personnel pawed through our scalps looking for lice, then worked their way over other parts of our anatomy down to our feet to where they had us spread our toes to expose any crud.

The fellow next to me milked down his "pecker." It oozed pus. He got a draft deferment. The doctor moved on down the line. In his bored tone I could hear him droning on, "Milk it down, spread your cheeks" and so on. Then he gasped, "My God!" The bottom of the foot of a huge black man was burned black, oozing juice like a freshly cooked steak. Molten iron in a Bethlehem mill had jumped a trench and caught his foot, burning through his shoe and skin into the muscle. He had not reported the accident for fear of losing his job.

When I was a kid, the family would occasionally visit my uncle at his summer home on the south shore of Lake Erie, about 20 miles west of Buffalo. To get there, we would have to pass through Lackawanna, home of the huge Bethlehem Steel plant. The road cut between the steel mill and a company housing project, the mill on the right along Lake Erie, the housing project to the left. In the summer, the mill's huge doors were opened allowing us to see the glow from molten metal and bursts of fire when blast furnaces were opened. The terrible heat seemed to engulf even those of us riding by in a car.

Sometimes we would pass as a shift was changing. Hordes of men carrying lunch boxes, their faces blackened with soot, their coveralls filthy, would pour out of the plant and head for the company houses across the road — one-story duplexes, row after row of them strung out like corn in a field — all of them blackened by the smoke and cinders spewed from Bethlehem's chimneys. There wasn't a sign of a tree or a planting of any kind to dispel the gloom or give relief from the heat. As for something green, there wasn't even a weed growing, much less a blade of grass.

By way of contrast, we lived at the time in a nice little house on Auburn Avenue, which my father was glad to get during a housing shortage following World War I. Our street, along with Lancester, Cleveland, Highland, and other streets that ran off Delaware Avenue, formed a neighborhood where up-and-coming young couples, scions of Buffalo's well-to-do families, bought their first homes. Lawns were always mowed, houses were freshly painted, and Buffalo's glorious elms shaded the houses, keeping them cool in the summer.

If you could have been in my dad's Buick you would have seen me, a kid, gaping out the window transfixed as we drove past Bethlehem Steel, awed by the flow of men pouring forth from an inferno and making their way across the street to their ugly little houses. There was no talk in that Buick until we were ten miles past the mill. We had to get over the mood created by its scene.

What I didn't know of my America at the time would fill a book. During the war, John L. Lewis, head of the coal miner's union, a big, burly guy who growled his message with Shakespearean sentences, took his miners out on strike in the middle of the war, potentially crippling the production of vital war materials. I was appalled when I heard about this, and spouted off in an Army barracks, calling him a traitor to the country in time of war. With that, one of the nicest guys in the barracks, a fellow who was always reading what genteel folk called literature, tore into me. "You don't know a damn thing about what you're shooting your mouth over. My mom and pop came over from the old country, got jobs in the mines, and became slaves to mine owners. We lived in company houses in a fenced-in enclave. We had to buy everything from the company store where we were always kept in debt, always enslaved. Lewis broke that up and if the war is going to be used as an excuse to turn the clock back and get us by the gonads again, then by God winning the war isn't worth it for us. I'm for Lewis."

Most of the men standing around on that cold floor of the post office building in 1941 were sons of parents who had come over from the "old country" before and just after the First World War. They were Polish, German, Italian, Jewish, Irish. They called each other polacks, huns, wops, yids, spiks. Verlyn Klinkenborg in writing *The Last Fine Time,* a book about Polish immigrants settling in Buffalo at the beginning of the century, listed the factories where these people went to work. Among the many were Buffalo Forge and Pierce Arrow, and four of them — Niagara Machine and Tool Works, Lautz Brothers Soap Company, Heinz and Munschauer, and the Weyand Brewery — were owned by my grandparents or great-grandparents. But not that much of the money they made came down to me. My ancestral line to these industrial barons traces through the maternal side of my family, and when they killed the fatted calves, the women got the neck bones. My relatives drove Packards, Cadillacs, Pierce-Arrows, and Lincolns. We had a Buick, which was nothing to complain about. As things trickled down the line of inheritance, my father was handed Heinz and Munschauer, a manufacturer of wooden iceboxes, at the time electric refrigerators were coming in.

His factory was a friendly place, a family place, and the workers were nice to me when I visited. But it was more than that. My father was a decent guy, although not an aggressive businessman, certainly not like some of his more successful relatives who were, at times, mean and greedy. And he was struggling trying to make metal electric refrigerators in a factory full of woodworking machinery — difficult anytime, but by then the Depression was on. The business was run for the workers; Dad took no salary and there were certainly no dividends. On the good days he would say, "We got a big order; I can put twenty-five men to work."

We weren't rich; nevertheless, my heritage dictated the circles I would travel in. I went to all the debutante balls. You may be taken in by the late-night TV comics who play on the notion that Buffalo is a jerk-water place, but let me tell you about it in my time. Kate Butler's family, who owned the *Buffalo Evening News*, had a mansion on Delaware Avenue which was decorated with thousands of white roses for her debutante ball. A fountain played in the entrance foyer while we danced to the music of Benny Goodman. A four-bedroom house could have been built for the money they paid to get him there. At a party given by a family who owned a steel mill, orange trees were brought into the country club in the middle of the winter to give the place a springlike atmosphere. The full Paul Whiteman band, of what seemed like a hundred pieces, supplied the music. Name any of the big bands of the '30s — Eddie Duchin, Isham Jones, and all the rest — each family vied to get the most famous, to outdo the others. Invitations were extended not because of friendship, but from social lists. My name appeared on one because I attended Charlie Van Arnam's dancing school, where the elite gathered. I grew up wearing tails or a tuxedo.

The ingredients were in place for me to become a snob. If I didn't make the grade, it was because I was seldom invited to the exclusive little dinners that often preceded dancing school, a subtle way of letting me know I wasn't quite good enough to be at the top of the social ladder. We were Catholics, which just wasn't a blue-blood religion; in fact, it was looked down upon socially. Poor Peanuts Lehman of the Wildroot hair tonic company (a product he used liberally) made it only as far as Charlie Van Arnam's dancing school, seldom if ever to a debutante party. He was Jewish.

My father had a way of squashing social pretensions. Several times my picture appeared in the social section of the *Sunday Courier Express*, showing me sipping a cup of tea or chatting with one of Buffalo's richest debutantes. "John," Dad said, "has it ever crossed your mind that out on some farm someone is using the *Courier Express* in their outhouse?" That took the edge off things. And my father wouldn't send me to a prep school, certainly not to the elite Andover or Exeter or Hotchkiss — not to even to the local Nichol's school where the minor Buffalo aristocratic attended. Instead, I went to Lafayette High School, not a very good school, in a tough neighborhood. Then, when it came time to go to college, I attended Cornell, the "cow college of the East," not a social institution like Yale.

I was kind of glad to be taken down a peg. I really didn't like dancing school or my social life very much. The conversation at parties was stupid, at least for me, because I was out of the loop of the truly elite who bantered little "in" jokes that were apparently hilarious to those who knew what was going on. And although the debutante parties were shows not to be missed, as was the view of the life of the upper crust, they were focused on but a tiny part of the social spectrum, and I needed a wider view.

In my time as now, we went to college and we got summer jobs to get a leg up on a career, and we paid lip service to opening our minds through our studies. Upton Sinclair and John Steinbeck were good reading, so we got all the sociological awareness we felt we needed from them. If you had asked, I would have told you I was a fairly democratic guy. Little did I realize how circumscribed my life actually was. I was a moth within a cocoon that hadn't been broken open for me to see what there was to see. But the Army was about to stomp on that cocoon and smash it open.

Rich or poor, down in that coal bin of the old post office, all of us were rabble. In the early days of the military draft before we entered the Hitler war, most men with a background like mine got a commission in the Navy or a draft-deferred job in a war plant. Anyone halfway up the blue-collar ladder had skilled jobs and worked in defense production. I, an "executive trainee" with the National Gypsum Company, a non-defense company where I planned to become a *Man in the Grey Flannel Suit*, was trapped when I drew a low number in the draft. And, stupidly believing Roosevelt's promise that men who were drafted would have to serve for only a year, I opted to serve as an enlisted man instead of getting a commission, which would have committed me to a four-year stint. Down in the bowels of that old post office, being shoved around like cattle, I would have given a fortune to be able to move back the calendar to get that commission.

Chapter 2

Cocoons

*N*ONE OF US in the post office dungeon had much to say to each other. There wasn't much chance to talk anyway, herded as we were from one waiting line to another, one for shots, another for an X-ray ("Take a deep breath and hold it"), then on to read an eye chart. Mostly, nobody felt like talking. Some of the biggest, toughest-looking bruisers were already showing signs of homesickness. Many of these men had never been out of the state, some hardly out of their neighborhood, and more than one had never slept in a house other than their own.

Later, in the bus for the 30-mile, two-hour ride to Fort Niagara, where we would spend our first night in the Army, men began to open up. First a bit of bravado from loudmouths with pointless dirty jokes to liven things up; the forced laughter from those who thought they ought to laugh egged them on. A few men found a friend to talk over the events of the miserable day. Others started to make new friends. A delicate young man who had been hanging near me glued himself to me to be sure we sat together on the bus. He needed a security blanket; he picked me.

He wanted to talk; I didn't. I wanted to switch my mind to neutral and stare out the window and watch the cars go by. But he wouldn't let me alone. Had I ever been away from home before? Did I think we would have our own rooms? He worried about food and listed at least ten he couldn't eat, not apparently because of any medical problems. He didn't like them, so his mother didn't serve them. Not only had he never been away from home before, but the only food he had ever eaten, except for church suppers, was "fixed the way he liked it" by his mom — hot cereal in the morning, a bag lunch for his noon break at the library where he shelved books, and a hot dinner at night. The two of them went to the Elmwood Theater every Friday evening for the 25-cent double feature and a free dinner plate, which they were collecting to make up a set. Saturdays, they went to museums; Sundays, to Sunday school, followed by an 11 o'clock service, and in the evening, vespers. Mommy was a widow and pretty well managed her son.

When he went nuts the next day at Fort Niagara, he had to be put in a room until he could be taken to a hospital. He asked for me to be with him, so I got the job of guarding him until professional help arrived. "They're after me," he kept saying. I asked him what made him think so. He said, "Can't you hear them whistling?" I hadn't heard anyone whistling, but after he mentioned it, it seemed everyone that walked down the hall past the room was whistling. I began to fear his problem was contagious, but I wasn't about to lose my mind — not even after the distasteful experiences at the post office induction. Besides the venereal disease, some of the men around me stunk. Most people bathed only once a week, and Saturday night was bath night, if the house had a tub. Some lived in flats with none, and a few had no hot water — just a sink with a cold-water tap. Showers were a luxury. Our little hose at 794 Auburn Avenue had had a tub, and then in 1937, my father, with many of his financial troubles behind him, bought a house on Morris Avenue that featured a tub *and* a shower, more befitting this son who was getting invited to the mansions of Buffalo's rich girls. In my little world, people took showers before going anywhere. I had taken one before reporting to the draft board, but I soon stunk from the cold sweat of suffering through the ordeal in the post office basement. Today, garbage man or banker, nobody would have stunk, thanks to the miracle of modern chemistry that created the deodorant.

For me, going into the Army was as much a breaking out of a cocoon as it was for the poor fellow whose mind had cracked in trying to get out of his. We were just raised in different cocoons. As a kid I, too, would walk to the Elmwood theater on Saturday afternoons, joining friends along the way until a huge stream of us, gathered from all the surrounding streets and avenues, descended on the Elmwood. On sunny Saturday afternoons, my mother would ask, "How can you coop yourself up inside a dark old theater on a beautiful afternoon like this?"

My mother couldn't know the thrill of being in the theater, screaming and hollering with hundreds of other kids to cheer the brave and good Tarzan as he tried to save Jane and her noble ape companion from evil hunters. How could she know? When she was growing up, there were no movies. I grew up in the age of the kids' Saturday afternoon movie, a golden era killed by television.

There was always something to enrich the life of a kid on Auburn Avenue, where we lived during the '20s and '30s. Houses had iceboxes instead of refrigerators. When the iceman delivered, he would chip off a few small pieces for the neighborhood kids. And the Hall's Bakery man would give us a little hay to feed his horse. Horsepower — real horsepower, not engine horsepower — provided the push to deliver our milk, our bread, our ice, and much of our produce. The smartest horse belonged to Jones' Dairy — "You can't beat our milk, but you can whip our cream." Without commands, he would make his way down the street, stopping at houses with a sign in a front window indicating that people needed milk.

Life in our little house at number 794 was serene. It was secure. We were kept from knowing that financial chaos hung over us during the depths of the Depression. My father, a director of a nearly insolvent savings and loan bank, walked the floor many nights worrying the bank might fail. But unlike today, when directors can mismanage with impunity, if his had failed, his money would have been seized and his home sold to pay off the depositors. Yet all I knew was a loving family.

My parents didn't fight. They had a rich social life. They were Re-
publicans. They were healthy. (My mother lived to be over 100.) I was
healthy. I didn't miss a day of school until I was 16, when I had my
appendix out. I thought everyone's life went along as serenely as mine.

After high school, I went to college. I loved college. I loved my fraternity. I loved the football games and singing victory songs in the bars
after the game. I had a wonderful education. It paid off. I got a job as an
executive trainee at $80 a month with the National Gypsum Company. I
would soon earn the the price ($700) of a coveted new Ford V8. I had it
made. But now all of that was down the drain. Now I, and a garbage
man, and a fisherman, and a tout, and a laborer, and a bank teller, and a
Mafioso, and a man who worked on an ore boat, and a drunk, and the
man who went crazy — the whole lot of us — stood in that old coal bin
and raised our hands to take an oath accepting an offer from the United
States Army we couldn't refuse. We were the sorriest-looking men anyone would pick to do any kind of a job, but we were in the vanguard of
millions like us to come who were to crush Hitler and Hirohito.

Miraculously, the next day — "shit, shaved, showered, and shined," as
the Army saying goes, with our hair cut short and our civilian clothes
replaced by a uniform — we looked like we could do it. Goodbye zoot
suits. Goodbye gray flannel suit. Goodbye greasy hair. Goodbye white
shirt. Goodbye blue shirt. Goodbye to anything that told which side of
the tracks we came from. Goodbye to anything to help us stereotype
each other. We saw each other as individuals. And as we were made to
look alike, we gained, rather than lost, an identity. Men began talking to
those they might never have before. Complaints about the Army became
the common theme that started us talking. From being stripped naked in
the bowels of the post office where we felt like plucked chickens, to
being outfitted in new uniforms, we became more in a mood to strut like
peacocks.

Now that we looked alike, the Army set about to find how we differed.
Were there among us mechanics, truck drivers, typists, soldiers with useful skills that the Army could use? We filled out forms. Forms were read.
The Army learned which of us could drive a truck, wire a telephone, or
blow a bugle. Then there was the tough question: Who were the smart
ones among us that could be trained as administrators or specialists? A
man's school record didn't always tell all the Army needed to know.

Many men smart enough to get a doctorate did not go to college in those days. Were there in this rabble men bright enough to learn the languages of the lands where we might fight? Were there men who might be able to master the mathematics involved in firing complicated artillery or to work in cryptography? Bright men had to be identified for positions of leadership. Men were given IQ tests, and some were surprised to learn they were smart. The tests were crude and in many cases unfair, but for sorting out large numbers, they worked. From the steel mills, from the factories, from the department stores, from the poor and the rich, the Army identified a pool of men to be slotted for positions of leadership.

While the Army was sorting us out, we were doing the same. First to find kindred souls were the crap shooters drawn by the sound of dice rolling on the barracks floor. Talk about women and boozing drew some together and drove away the mom, apple pie, and the girl left behind crowd. Cars, baseball, books, and music were affinity subjects. In civilian life, economic and social barriers kept men from finding each other; in the service there were no such barriers. An unemployed artist from a family living on the dole found a friend in an heir to a pharmaceutical fortune who loved art. Discovering they were Yankee fans brought together a Princeton graduate and a high school drop-out. A singer who had been selected to audition for the Metropolitan Opera found much in common with a department store clerk who loved opera.

The singer and the artist and the clerk were to become my friends, as well as the future funeral director, whose quiet manner already reflected reassurance. His face, with its built-in sadness and its hypnotic eyes, could surely calm the most hysterical widow. Before being drafted, he had started his career as a bank teller to please his mother. All the ingredients were in place for the story of a tragic life: a 31-year-old bachelor locked in a stifling job, living at home with a domineering mother, stuck in a small town where everybody knew more than they ought to know about everybody else. People like him seemed to seek me out. Maybe it's because I look clean. A friend of mine in college said I could come in full of mud from a football game and still look clean! In any event, our funeral director had selected me to hear yet another sad story of a man tied to his mother's apron strings, this time for what became the beginning of a lasting friendship. He told his story with a twinkle in his eye. He could describe his situation in the abstract and make it seem like a very funny soap opera about a bachelor in a small town. Like all people with a sense of humor, he made a good friend.

Where else would I have found such a friend, other than as an enlisted man in the Army? Where else but in the Army would we — a garbage man, a tout, a fisherman, a trainee in a corporate program, and so many other different kinds of men — have been thrown together to make such unlikely but wonderful friends? Where else would we have been able to break open our tightly spun cocoons, with different cultural threads, and discover that, for the most part, Americans were decent and intelligent? Elites — the highly educated, especially those who are very liberal or very conservative — who have never had such an experience, think they know what is best for everyone. They try to impose their ideas on others because they do not trust the intelligence and integrity of the average person. In 1941, I would have given a fortune to have escaped the draft, but if anything was worth a fortune, it was to be drafted. I came into the Army full of prejudices and I probably would have kept them if I had been an officer. But as an enlisted man, they soon got knocked out of me.

The common misery of being drafted was a catalyst for friendship, but it was the uniform that broke the barriers to friendship. "Birds of a feather flock together," but if the feathers are different, birds stay away from each other.

As an employment counselor after the war, I often called on employers. I recall visiting the Orbach's store on 14th Street in New York as the guest of the personnel director, Mary Sable. Orbach's bought clothes from famous designers, had them copied, then priced them as bargains, which brought customers flocking. The place was a madhouse; in some aisles it was impossible to get through, as people fought to get at the merchandise. I remarked that it wouldn't be worth the effort for me to push through such a mob to find a bargain. Mary smiled and said, "And don't think the clerks haven't noticed you as the type of person who disdains grubbing for bargains. Instinctively they have you sized up as someone out of their class, possibly a physician or a professor, or even a rich sportsman. In fact they don't like you."

I asked why.

"It's your clothes. You're wearing a sport coat; these people wear suits. Your pants aren't pressed; theirs are. And your shoes belong on the Appalachian Trail more than in New York City. But mostly it's your sport coat. It's beautiful. It's the real thing, not a copy. They know it cost a fortune."

My daughter had seen the sport coat in a thrift shop that sold second-hand clothes for the benefit of a charity, liked it, and bought it for me.

An Army uniform gave us all the same feathers and it served us well in helping us find friends before we were sidetracked by a false impression. But sometimes feathers like those of a peacock get their colors more from light refraction than pigment. Unfortunately, I lost a good Army buddy when he saw me once in a different light. When we first met, we had hit it off immediately. We liked to go drinking at the Post Exchange or in town — nothing wild, just good conversation and joke telling over a pitcher of beer. Our outfit was moved to Fort Dix near his home. He had been given a weekend pass to visit his family and wanted me to join him. I had already gotten a pass to visit a friend who happened to live in his town. We worked it out so that I would spend Saturday and Sunday morning with him, and after dinner Sunday I would transfer to my other friend.

My first buddy's family was poor, that was readily apparent, and from something I heard his mother whisper to his father, probably on welfare. Furthermore, there was a brother "in the attic," put there so I could have his room. The brother did not eat with us. A best foot was being put forward for my sake, and the odd brother didn't fit their plan to make a good impression for their son's friend. For Sunday dinner they went all out, serving a pot roast with cocktails before, warm whiskey in warm ginger ale in a house heated to at least 95 degrees, possibly hot enough for the heat to drift upstairs to the brother. It was bitterly cold outside. My friend's sister, along with her loudmouthed husband, joined us for dinner. He was a union man through and through — more than that really, a communist in spirit if not in fact. All I heard during the whole meal was a harangue about the dirty capitalist, how the manufacturers were squeezing labor for profits. I thought of my father struggling to keep his business going during the Depression.

The college friend I was to visit next lived in another section known as "the mountain," where some of the homes overlooked New York City. I knew my humbler friend's family did not have a car and I had planned to take a taxi, but "loudmouth" had unexpectedly showed up with a vehicle and insisted he drive me. I tried hard to say "no thanks," but without luck. He, his wife, my friend, and his dad piled in the car. As we got closer and the road began to make its way up the mountain, the houses got bigger, and "loudmouth" got louder. I began to freeze in my seat. I had heard that my college friend's home was big. Little did I know how big. When we got to the right street number, there was a gate house. I should have gotten off there, telling them something like, "I'm supposed to walk to the house and look for my friend along the way; he'll be working in a garden." But, no, I couldn't think of anything. So we drove up a winding lane. At the top there wasn't a house, there was a castle. "Loudmouth," subdued, said something about waiting to see if this was the right place. A butler opened the door and took my suitcase. I turned and waved goodbye, and goodbye to a friendship that was never the same again. My humble companion had been humiliated. And in a kind of guilt by association, he now had me typed as another kind, not the ordinary fellow he was comfortable with.

Fort Niagara, having finished with us, loaded us on a troop train for a slow trip south. We were constantly shunted to sidings to let the freight trains barrel through that were loaded with steel and coal and chemicals to feed the factories gearing up to a wartime economy. As we ambled along through the countryside, occasionally passing through towns where some of the men on board were from, people gathered along the track with flags to wave us on, and I couldn't help but think of Lincoln's funeral train. I had a feeling we were caught up in some kind of a parade, a cavalcade, something that was going to be very big. Something stirred inside. I felt the urge to march. I had to remind myself to hate Roosevelt and his draft.

Chapter 3

Bedpans and OR

WE WERE HEADING south, that was all we knew. Nobody told us where we were going. Nobody ever told anybody anything in the Army, hence soldiers thrive on rumors. Proof that we were already soldiers lay in the rumors that started traveling from car to car; the most persistent and the one that proved to be right was that we were headed for Fort Bragg, North Carolina. Adding to the speculation was the arrival of a captain who climbed aboard the second day and holed up with a sergeant in a room at the end of a sleeping car. Rumor had it that they were about to arrest someone for trying to desert. Another, based on someone noticing the captain and the men with him wore a caduceus, the symbol of the Medical Corps, was that we were going to be given more shots.

On arrival, ten or so buses were waiting at the Fort Bragg railroad siding. Thirty names, mine among them, were called and told to load into the first vehicles. The mysterious captain got into a staff car and drove off. Our bus followed, passing areas of scrub pine and sand being cleared to convert Fort Bragg, once a small and beautiful old Army post, into a modern training facility for an Infantry division. We were unloaded in the old and still attractive part of Fort Bragg in front of an impressive brick barracks with porches in the rear at each level — my first home in the Army. Most draftees started their Army life in temporary wooden buildings like those in the new part of Fort Bragg where most of the men on our train were taken. Across the way from our barracks, however, separated by a well-mowed parade ground, was a cluster of other pleasing-looking buildings, nicely landscaped with shrubbery and flowers. Old Fort Bragg looked more like a college campus than a military post. The new part out in the scrub pines housed the 9th Infantry Division. New wooden barracks had been built and were still being thrown up on the grassless sand of the area amongst pines and chigger bugs.

The captain, Captain Dear, had scored a coup by boarding the train, sorting through the records of the passengers, and picking men who were well educated or had scored well on the Army's intelligence test. With outstanding men, he was well on his way to making a success of his new command, the 66th General Hospital, a unit formed to train enlisted men for hospital duty as either medical technicians or clerks. The 66th might better have been designated a medical administrative and technicians school, as it had no patients, doctors, or nurses. But should a war come, the men of the 66th would be combined with doctors in a reserve unit to form a new hospital capable of treating patients.

I should have been thrilled to join the medics. No branch of the service, indeed of the entire government, has a more illustrious history. Army surgeon Walter Reed's findings relative to the transmission of malaria and yellow fever alone places the medical department at the forefront of medical and military achievement. The earliest inclination of the importance of cholesterol was discovered by Army pathologists during World War II. During every war, the practice of medicine has been advanced by the Medical Corps. Further, military medicine was in my family history. My grandfather was a surgeon's assistant in the Navy during the Civil War. Because he died in 1890, six days after my father's birth, the information we have on him is brief, but we do know that he was eventually discharged because of stomach problems that were aggravated, we understand, by the terror he felt assisting in operations or limb amputations performed with little or no anesthesia. But I was not in a mood to reflect on history or my ancestry.

Captain Dear was a second-generation Regular, a member of the old Army; his father was General Dear. The name Dear lent itself to disparaging remarks when things didn't go well for us, just one of many plays on the name that probably plagued the family, but at least they were better off than a gentleman by the name of Hospital, who became a general. He complained of never-ending trouble with telephone operators switching calls meant for him to the hospital. And there was Major Clancy, who was a private. His name drove our First Sergeant nuts. "Damn it Clancy, stop calling yourself Major, you're a private!" The sergeant, an Army old-timer, couldn't get it through his head that Major was a given name. "Major, by God, was a name that belonged to the Army and no one had the right to use it, especially a damned civilian!"

In this and so many things there was no reasoning with the old-time Regular Army men who were to dominate our lives in the early months of our training. Jones, in his book *From Here to Eternity,* portrayed these men well. They lived in a thoroughly corrupt and thoroughly fascinating cocoon all their own. I was always glad, however, that I entered the Army enough before the war to experience their colorful culture before we civilian draftees arrived in droves, overwhelming them and their way of life.

The 66th General Hospital had its share of screwups, and Dear, as the commander, naturally was blamed. We didn't understand. He was basically a medical doctor, perhaps even a brilliant surgeon, but like a good soldier, he did his duty; he sacrificed a love for his medical practice to form a hospital training unit. In the old Army tradition, where sergeants were the administrators, an officer could be a figurehead and strut around looking important in his uniform, something like British royalty. But this could hardly have been the case with Dear. We had no idea what he was up against. There was probably no standard procedure for starting a new unit such as the 66th. Undoubtedly, he had to design the training program. Liaison had to be established with the Fort Bragg Post Hospital to arrange for some of us to be detailed there for training. But we had no appreciation for this. We only saw what affected our lives: cleaning an already clean barracks, unfair pass policies, sergeants meting out extra duty for imagined offenses. We knew that the sergeants were behind most of this, but we wondered if Captain Dear arrived in the morning, signed the orders his sergeants had prepared for him, and took off for a golf game. Sometimes it looked like that was the way the 66th was run.

I had a college education, and, even more importantly, I could type. That should have qualified me for an administrative assignment, which was where the promotions were, not from the bedpan brigade on the wards, where the best to be hoped for was a promotion to private first class. But I was assigned to the bedpan brigade. It was my own fault. During training, before any job assignments, in addition to hours on end of being drilled on the Army way to turn left, turn right, and turn around, we attended orientation lectures that included instruction in anatomy and physiology, a new and difficult subject for most of the trainees, but not for me. Not long before I had taken a course in anatomy at Cornell, and wanting to show the Army I was smart, I drew on this knowledge to breeze through the final anatomy exam with a perfect score. Having displayed this knowledge, where else did I think I would be assigned?

We, the chosen men of the bedpan brigade, were detailed to the Post Hospital, where there were real patients, sick soldiers, soldiers in surgery. We could work on them to become experts in giving enemas, making beds, washing patients, and shaving the genitals of men about to be operated on, mostly for appendicitis. Shaving was a hated chore, but like most unpleasant hospital tasks, it's one you get used to.

Our duties at the hospital began at 7:00 a.m. and ended at 7:00 p.m., or the other way around if we happened to be on the night shift. The shifts changed on Monday with both crews working the full 24 hours, apparently the only way a sergeant (though we blamed Dear) could figure out to change shifts. With reveille already set at 5:30, to allow time for morning roll call, barracks cleaning, inspection, and breakfast, wake-up was soon moved to 5:00 a.m. to comply with an order sent down from the Surgeon General in Washington prescribing a minimum of 30 minutes of morning calisthenics. By 5:01, we were out in front of the barracks, jumping around like idiots in the middle of the night. Only those lucky guys on the night shift got out of this nonsense. Perhaps this was good training for what might come. Hospital staff in wartime frequently work these hours and more. But there is a price to pay. No one can keep up such a work load and remain alert and sharp — as I found out.

Work on the wards is literally "shitty." One poor devil had done it all over himself. Far too sick to even raise his head, much less to get up and go to the bathroom to clean himself, he pleaded for someone to wipe him clean. From one end of the ward to the other, the place stunk. The corpsman assigned to this patient took off. Thinking it wouldn't kill me, I wiped and washed the kid, a gentle and very sick and very scared hillbilly from the mountains of North Carolina. In tears of gratitude, he told me where to find his wallet and begged me to take a nickel for myself. I took it. It gave him something he could do for me. It gave him dignity. Fortunately none of the old-time Army officers ever heard that I had taken money from a patient. That being against regulations, I wouldn't expect them to do anything other than the right thing: court-martial me.

Serving meals to patients presented a challenge. Food delivered from the kitchen had to be transferred to trays in a pantry where cockroaches swarmed over the food like settlers charging into the opening of the Oklahoma Territory. Some patients were fussy about cockroaches with their food, but picking up a tray and banging it up and down on the counter scattered them. Quickly then, for the roaches wasted no time getting back, the tray had to be picked up and dashed to the patient.

Cleanliness on the ward was important. One night a sick prisoner under guard was carried in on a litter. For awhile the guard took his duty seriously, standing by the unconscious man with his rifle at the alert, very military-like, as if he had a prisoner of war about to make a dash for freedom. Gradually, seeing that patient couldn't even talk, much less walk, he began to relax, first shoving his rifle under the bed, then sitting down in a chair. Eyeing an empty bed, he decided to take a nap, dirty boots and all, on clean bedding. When I caught him in the act and told him he couldn't use the bed, he responded with the Army's most popular four-letter word. I wasn't offended, but simply told him, "OK, but two hours ago a soldier died in that bed and we like to keep beds free for awhile until the death vapors leave." As he retreated to where he belonged, the only thing that could have explained the peculiar look that came over his face was that he may have believed he already had inhaled the vapors!

Some of the men assigned as ward boys in the bedpan brigade couldn't stomach the patients' groans, wiping bottoms, and emptying stinking bedpans. Some were reassigned; some goldbricked — which is the Army art of doing nothing while looking like you are busy as hell. Most men found it harder to goldbrick than to pitch in and do the work. Less out of a sense of duty and more from a sense of numbness to our surroundings, we got through our 96-hour weeks working our tails off, and in the process became zombies. Medical students and interns reputedly work these kind of hours, getting as little or less sleep as we. I can't imagine a crazier way to train a doctor. The body keeps going, but the mind shuts down. A person becomes dangerous. I did, and I look back to the events as the worst day in my life.

In a private patient's room next to the nurse's station — one of three single rooms reserved for officers, but occasionally pressed into service for very sick enlisted men — a captain was due to get an enema prior to a proctoscopy examination. The job fell to me. There was no urgency, so I finished cleaning up several patients and prepared another for surgery, then headed for the fatal room with my enema kit. Seeing that the captain was too ill to use a toilet, I shoved a bedpan under him and started the enema. I began to sense that something wasn't quite right. A proctoscopy exam on somebody this sick didn't quite fit. I looked at the chart. It listed his rank as "*Private* . . . Appendicitis, ruptured."

Oh, God! An enema was the worst possible thing for him. Enough gangrenous pus was dumping out of his ruptured appendix into his abdomen without adding fluid from an enema. I thought I was going to get sick. The arteries leading to my brain pounded. His chance to live was already slim, and now I had surely sealed his doom. I thought of putting a tube in his rectum and trying to suck out the fluid. I called a nurse. She called a physician. They said what was done was done. While they didn't excuse me, they didn't accuse me. The physician actually praised me for owning up to my mistake, noting that I could have covered it up. For half a second, I had thought about doing that.

I stayed with the private and nursed him until he died a few days later. Joining me at his bedside were his mother and father — wonderful highly cultured Jewish people, who found some comfort in their religion.

Unfortunately, in delirium, the son called his mother foul names and yelled obscenities at his father. Such totally irrational behavior was not unusual, and in no way should be interpreted as indicative of their son's true feelings, according to the physician in charge of the case. The parents understood. They had to understand. They stayed through the ordeal with dignity and compassion. And probably my enema did not hasten death; only penicillin could have saved his life. But it was 1941 — there was no penicillin.

Sometimes tragedy brings matters to a head. My performance as a medic was reviewed. Note was taken of the hours I worked, of my exhaustion. Nurses spoke up for me. Owning up to my mistake earned me the most points. Instead of punishment, I was offered a chance to try out for a better and interesting job in surgery. For the test, four soldiers and I donned operating-room gowns and were led by a nurse into a room where a patient, already anesthetized, was about to undergo surgery. It struck me that our white gowns and hats made us look like ghosts. I pictured the patient half waking up and seeing us through the the fog of anesthesia and jumping off the table.

That crazy thought passed, and I settled down to watch. The surgeon held up his rubber-gloved hand; a nurse beside him slapped a scalpel into it. He made a cut across the patient's skin, then a second to go deeper. An artery squirted a thin stream of blood into the air like water from a garden hose. Before anyone could catch him, one of the ghosts hit the floor. Of the five of us, he seemed the least likely to pass out; he was an embalmer in civilian life. Embarrassed, he later admitted that he thought nothing of draining blood from an artery, but when it squirted from a live body, he couldn't take it. Blood from someone alive was as horrifying to him as blood from a corpse would be for me.

A large incision was opened into the chest cavity, and the nurse, staying one step ahead of the operation, handed the surgeon a large instrument that looked like tree-pruning shears, the kind with long handles and short blades that have lots of leverage. Working the blades over a rib, the surgeon squeezed. Crunch went the rib. Two more ghosts hit the floor.

Only J. C. Thornberg from North Carolina and I were standing. We had passed the initial screening. Next an interview.

What did we think of the operation? I confessed to feeling dispassionate about what I saw, focusing my attention on what the surgeon was doing. My answer was just what they wanted. I was somebody who could concentrate on the operation and not the gore. I was assigned to the OR — operating room — along with J. C. Interestingly, if I were to happen across an accident where morbid onlookers were watching transfixed, I would have to turn away. If I could be useful, however, I could pitch in, feeling no more squeamish than if I would be working on my car. In fact, the operation made me think of carpentry and mechanics. The instruments would fit well into a carpenter's tool chest, especially the hemostat, a sort of pliers that can be locked to clamp off a bleeding artery. It would make a great tool for doing things like holding the end of a wire to free up hands for use elsewhere. Whoever invented the vise grip may have picked up the idea from seeing a hemostat.

An operation is like a play — the performance is the culmination of hours of preparation. The operating room is the stage. J. C. and I were to spend many hours as stage hands. The most-feared villain in the play is not the patient's broken bones, or his appendicitis, or his hernia, or whatever vile mishap has felled him; it is a microscopic bit of staphylococcus or streptococcus floating around the operating room on a piece of dust waiting to land on the patient, causing an infection. All too often, a small microbe floating on a piece of dust has turned a simple operation into a foul tragedy. As stage hands, our job was to wash down the operating room and its equipment so that these villains were not present. Should a known infection be brought into the room by a patient with a gangrenous leg, for example, everything in the room — the floor, the ceiling, the walls, the light fixtures,the operating table — had to be scrubbed with Lysol before the room could be used again. I got used to smelling of Lysol after a cleanup.

Everything necessary for an operation — scalpels, hemostats, scissors, clamps, retractors, sutures, needles — has to be arranged in a pack to be ready as needed and laid out in a logical order on a stand next to the surgeon. When a hemorrhage must be stopped, it's no time to be fumbling around, like looking for a nickel in a coin purse full of quarters, trying to find a hemostat in a jumble of other instruments. Packs have to be sterilized, as do bandages, sponges, water, linens, and such, all stored in quantity, for scheduled operations, as well as for an unexpected influx of cut and bruised soldiers following a Saturday night brawl in nearby Fayetteville. It was our job as stage hands to keep supplies ample and to keep them in well-labeled packs. A surgeon about to do brain surgery isn't going to be very happy if the pack he got contained instruments for an appendectomy.

I may have mixed up a patient, but never the instruments. Surgery is a place for discipline and discipline is what we got from the nurse in charge of the OR, a lieutenant from Kannapolis, North Carolina. Her real name, which has slipped my mind, should have been remembered to give her due praise for her management. Twenty-four-hour days happened in the operating room — a personnel carrier rolling over on maneuvers sending a dozen men to the hospital could throw off the schedule of the best-run operating room — but our nurse, unlike Captain Dear, saw that hours didn't get out of hand. She knew zombies didn't belong in an operating room. Let a colonel try to rearrange a schedule for his personal convenience and gyp an enlisted man of well-earned time off, and the colonel would soon learn what it was like to be put in his place by this soft-spoken lieutenant with a southern accent. My most fond memory is of Lieutenant Georgiana Niemeyer from Kalamazoo, Michigan, another highly competent operating room nurse. I liked her. One day I felt like grabbing her and giving her a big kiss, which I did. God forbid, the lips of an enlisted man touching an officer! Decidedly against regulations. God forbid Captain Dear finding out. Our lieutenant from Carolina, the disciplinarian, laughed. Today I'd be thrown in the guard house for sexual harassment.

If the U.S. entered the war, I would be shipped overseas to take charge of a field hospital operating room. That meant I had to learn scrub, which in surgery has nothing to do with washing walls and ceilings. It pertains to being a surgeon's assistant during an operation, managing the instruments and handing them to the surgeon as needed. It meant having my hands in the wound, sponging away blood blocking the surgeon's vision. It meant cutting sutures. It meant that I would have to become more of an assistant surgeon than just a scrub nurse.

Scrubbing is the antiseptic ritual to ensure the sterility of the hands and clothing of the operating crew. It begins with 20 minutes of scour-

ing the arms and hands with a harsh brush and coarse soap. Once finished, the water is drained away from the cleaned hands, and the arms
must be held up like the paws of a begging puppy dog, to ensure against
touching something, never to be dropped below the waist until the operation is over. Next, the surgeons and scrub nurse (from "scrubbed"
nurse) don sterile gowns and rubber gloves. Like Adam and Eve com-
manded by God not to touch the apple, surgeon and nurse must not touch
anything other than the instruments and the patient. And just as in the
Garden of Eden, Satan is present to destroy their resolve. He makes
noses itch. There is no torture like a nose itch, knowing it can't be
scratched.

Once I was tortured for five hours. A mess sergeant and his helper had
been working on an oven door trying to undo a rusted screw. With the
sergeant on one side of the door pushing the screwdriver hard to keep it
from slipping out of the screw head, and the helper on the other side
leaning against the door with his chest to provide an equal and opposite
force, the screwdriver slipped off the screw, past the edge of the door
into the helper's chest. A large needle on a syringe was pushed into the
chest cavity to draw out fluid for analysis to try to determine whether the
heart had been punctured, and finally determining that it had been, and
after trying various tactics to stop the bleeding without opening the
chest, the surgeon finally decided he had to go in and examine the heart.
The torn heart had to be sewed together. Throughout the ordeal, nose
itches came and went. We tried various unsuccessful facial grimaces,
thinking they might help. Actual scratching is available from a nurse
who stands at the ready for such things, whose usual job is only to wipe
sweat from the surgeon's brow to keep it from dripping into the patient.
In hot North Carolina, before the days of air conditioning, the tempera-
ture in the operating room sometimes rose above 100 degrees. During
this operation, I asked to have my nose scratched, but no one can satis-
factorily scratch another's nose. After four hours into our work, I did get
another kind of help, some sustenance from a glass of milk held for me
to drink through a straw. And, fortunately, in a few days, the patient,
with stitches in his heart, was running all over the hospital having a great
time.

Saturday night is a soldier's night for raising hell, and a busy night in
the operating room. A soldier who had had more than his share of rev-

elry was brought in one evening with a mangled hand, apparently run over by a freight train, as he was found lying by the tracks in the Fayetteville rail yards. But he was either too drunk to tell us or in too much shock to know. He claimed he had drunk only two beers. Saturday night patients always claimed they had had two beers; never more, never less.

Luckily for the soldier, Captain Thiessen, a surgeon trained at the Mayo Clinic, was on duty. If anyone could do the right thing by that hand, it would be Thiessen. Not only was he the most skilled surgeon in the surgical service, but the most thoughtful toward the patient, and those of us who worked for him. During an operation, he would explain what he was doing, why he was using a hemostat, or a scalpel, or whatever. Each operation was a lesson in anatomy and physiology. But he couldn't do much with the man's hand except clean it up and get the soldier ready to send to Walter Reed Hospital in Washington for specialized treatment. Yet just preparing the patient for a specialist would have to be done with great delicacy. The Captain worked 20 minutes trying to protect a thin strand of flesh connected to an almost severed finger. That bit of tissue, he explained, might be vital to saving the finger. He searched for nerves and blood vessels that might be saved. While some surgeons might have sloshed the hand with peroxide and slapped on some stitches in a 20-minute fix, Thiessen worked on it from midnight until four in the morning to save as much tissue as possible for a hand surgeon to use in an attempt at restoration. A hand surgeon? How specialized can medicine get? Seeing that tangle of nerves and muscles and tendons and cartilage and skin, I had the answer. If anything ever happens to my hands I am going to a hand surgeon. It's asking too much for the average general surgeon to deal with such complex anatomy.

Other than something very specialized like hand or nerve surgery where I would want a specialist, if ever I had to have an operation, I knew that Thiessen was the man I wanted. Yet among the soldiers in the wards, Thiessen came away a poor second to another surgeon who was handsome and "full of bull." Most appendectomies were performed under a spinal anesthetic, which meant the patient was conscious. This swashbuckling surgeon took full advantage of the patient as an audience, with a running dialogue designed to please. When a fully inflamed and swollen appendix is exposed, it pops right out; one that is not infected hangs off the intestine like a small worm. No matter what the size, the brazen surgeon had the same line, "Wow! Look at that. About to burst. Never seen one bigger. Caught it just in time."

Of course the patient loved it. Everyone likes to brag about his operation, and, as the soldiers saw it, this man had saved their lives. Naturally they loved him. Furthermore, their scars were hardly two inches long! That was something to talk about. To listen to the patients, the smaller the scar and the quicker the operation, the better the surgeon. Unfortunately, Captain Thiessen left a longer scar. The guys on the ward who had Thiessen felt let down.

Patients didn't know the down side of small incisions. The bravado surgeon's assistants had to insert retractors, a flat instrument bent at the end like a hook, over the edge of the incision and pull like crazy to stretch the opening. Frequently, at the surgeon's urging, I had to pull so hard I had to put my foot on the base of the operating table to keep from sliding. I was afraid the patient was going to split wide open. Sometimes an appendix can be hard to find, especially a healthy little wormlike appendage. And this surgeon's patients had appendages that were often hard to find. Captain Thiessen's, however, were seldom a problem because he was a better diagnostician. In any event, with an elusive appendix, a wide opening makes it easier to search for the culprit. Thiessen's larger incisions let him examine a large segment of the intestines, which he did whether the appendix was inflamed or not. Once while I was scrubbing he found a malignancy, another time a Meckle's diverticulum — a kind of large wart growing on the intestine that can cause as much or more trouble than an appendix.

During maneuvers, with war games spread over half of North Carolina, ambulatory patients were gathered in the field at medical aid stations and brought by bus to the Fort Bragg Hospital. Rumor had it that our charismatic surgeon had met the buses to line up patients to practice his 15-minute appendectomy, his 18-minute hernia repair, and his 10-minute hemorrhoidectomy. When this handsome man with his great personality, a good line, and his mastery of the short incision returned to civilian life after the war, all the ingredients would be in place to attract a large, high-paying society practice.

The trick in an appendectomy is to cut the appendix loose from the intestine and not let its foul contents and pus spill into the abdomen. The abdominal wall is lined with a membrane called the peritoneum, a tissue where infection spreads like a forest fire in a high wind. To cut off the appendix in a way that prevents pus from leaking, the surgeon places two clamps side by side at its base and cuts between them. The appendix, its amputated end clamped shut, can then be lifted out of the abdomen without spilling any pus. The remaining stump, still clamped, is cauterized to keep it sealed after the remaining clamp is removed. It's logical, something a surgeon — a master plumber and carpenter at heart — would figure out to do if he hadn't learned the procedure in training.

Yet my faith in the medical profession was shaken more than once. During an appendectomy at which I was assisting, the surgeon clamped the base of the appendix with two clamps as he should, then wondered aloud where he should cut. With that he positioned his scalpel next to a clamp by the intestine instead of between the clamps. Though just a private, I started to yell, "No, Doctor, cut between the clamps!" But too late. The surgeon made the wrong cut, leaving a gaping hole in the wall of the intestine.

In another infamous operation, a red-nosed, red-faced orthopedic surgeon — we called him "Shaky" — was trying to repair a fractured leg. To keep a bone steady while he drilled some holes in it for screwing on a plate, he had me bend a pliable soft metal instrument called a ribbon retractor to fit behind the bone. After a few minutes of drilling, it seemed to me he had drilled through the bone, so I told him so. No response. Shaky turned the crank of his drill faster and kept going. Louder, but very respectfully because I was only a private and he a colonel, I said, "I think you're through the bone, Doctor." Still no response. Metal shavings began to appear. He had drilled through the retractor, and now the bit was stuck in it. To remove it, he gave a big heave, sending him back off balance, swinging him around so the bit hit me in the face. Recovering, he repositioned the drill about to enter the wound to bore another hole. I mentioned that he had hit me in the face with the drill.

"I'm sorry," he said and started back to drill again.

"No," I tried to tell him, "when the drill hit my face it became contaminated. It's no longer sterile."

He mumbled as he sloshed a little alcohol on the bit, then continued the operation. Unfortunately, like the peritoneum, bone is especially susceptible to infection. A little alcohol could not have sterilized that drill.

If ever I needed an orthopedic surgeon, I was determined not to have old Shaky. And in time, I was equally determined to have another doctor whose name I no longer can recall — a great surgeon. Unfortunately, I would have had the devil's own time getting him then. He was, as we called black men at the time, colored, and colored surgeons, either from custom or possibly by directive, did not operate on white patients. Usually two medical doctors — a surgeon, and an assistant surgeon — performed an operation, but if the doctor available to assist was colored and the patient was white, I or J. C. would be selected to assist instead. To be honest — in the frame of mind of the times, at the outset of my induction and training — if I, as a white boy, were to undergo surgery, and one of the doctors who was going to cut me open was colored, I would have been scared to death. It was 1941 and an entirely different world. Yet I would learn that being smart was a matter of cranial cells, not melanin. Working in the operating room, I learned that some colored doctors were competent and some were not, and some white doctors were competent and some were not.

Surgery — the drama of the operating room, my image of the surgeon as a paragon — was turning out to be far different from what I had expected. Certainly it was nothing like the way it's dramatized by Hollywood with Dr. Wonderful operating in a desperate effort to save a life.

Most operations at Fort Bragg were fairly routine, and there was little of the dramatic "sponge, clamp, scalpel" dialogue. Scrub nurses, anticipating a surgeon's every move, would have an instrument ready to place in his hand without him having to ask for it. Soon I could figure out what needed to be done and would have the right instrument ready at the right time. Thus operations proceeded in silence, or with light conversation about who pitched yesterday's game for the Yankees. The exception was a particular surgeon, a clown, who, when operating on hemorrhoids where the patient was under a spinal anesthetic, and therefore conscious, used to go through the routine of "scissors, scalpel, sponge," the whole bit in a high theatrical voice to provide drama; then for the climax, practically shouting, he would say, "REAMER!" The patient's eyes would almost pop out of his head. Of course there was no such thing as a reamer, but after the anesthetic wore off the patient thought there was.

Some surgeons are instrument throwers. We had one; the nurses told me they were not uncommon. No matter what the instrument handed to

"Dr. Petulant," he would toss it aside. Then, like a bull in a china shop, he would paw over the instrument tray, thoroughly messing up the systematic way things were laid out. When he finally found what he wanted, it would be the same as the one he had rejected. He was like some people in restaurants who always send their order back to the kitchen because it isn't hot enough, the meat is too raw, or too well done!

The more tense the operation, the more this doctor's perturbation. The more his perturbation, the more he grabbed for instruments. The more he grabbed for instruments, the more he he messed up the system. The more he messed up the system, the more the delays in finding instruments. He would get himself into what my grandmother used to call a tizzy. I suffered through one of his tizzies. During an operation that started as a simple appendectomy, everything went wrong, including a missing appendix. It was eventually found on the left side of the abdomen instead of the right where it belongs (unusual, but nothing like the young draftee in the 66th who became our first sergeant, whose heart, liver, the works, everything was reversed). Because the operation wasn't proceeding along the usual lines, I began anticipating the doctor's needs, including a special suture that I started to thread. Noticing me from the corner of his eye, he grabbed the needle, took the suture, and aimed for its eye. Missed. No luck on the next try either, or the next. I took the needle and thread from him and calmly ran the suture through the eye on the first try.

Medical anomalies were not uncommon. An exploratory operation on a frail lad to investigate peculiar symptoms revealed an undeveloped set of ovaries. Dr. Thiessen turned him into a complete man. Another soldier was troubled by an unusually large penis, attributed not so much to virility as to a suspected growth, the latter proving to be the case — fortunately benign.

With few exceptions, operations below the diaphragm were performed under a spinal anesthetic. Patients were placed on their side in the fetal position while the anesthetist inserted a hypodermic needle between vertebrae through which he injected a novocaine-like anesthetic into the spinal column, paralyzing the patient from the waist down. Nobody likes even the tiniest needle stuck in their arm or butt, much less a large one tapped into their spinal column. A few patients trembled, making it hard for the anesthetist to get a good tap. At the slightest prick some would holler and squirm, not a good thing to do with a breakable needle in the spinal column. If the needle touched a nerve, a foot might twitch, making it difficult to keep the patient still. A corpsman always wrapped his arms around the legs and head of the patient, locking hands together to hold the patient in the fetal position, a grip I doubt any of us could hold if the patient decided to straighten out. Fortunately, most were more than content to have us hold them. The fetal position was the next best thing to the security of their mother's womb, which no doubt is where they would like to have been at that point.

Chapter 4

Broken Promise

*I*NITIALLY, DRAFTEES could tell how many more days they had before their year of service was up; then Franklin Roosevelt reneged on his promise to draft for just a year. Troops felt betrayed. A movement started among the troops called OHIO, for Over the Hill In October. "Over the hill" was a euphemism for desertion; October was the end of the year for the first men to be drafted. Trucks were painted with the slogan, but the rebellion was just talk, talk that gave the military brass sleepless nights. I wasn't happy to have my enlistment extended, but if I was to be stuck in the military, my life had settled into a good pattern. My job was interesting, the hours reasonable, and my pay above average, $56 a month instead of the $30 for an ordinary private. I was promoted to private first class and, in addition, given a technical rating that boosted my pay still further — by $10 or so. I bought the Ford V8 I had planned to get as a civilian. Privates were not allowed to have cars, but with a little support from the officers in the surgical group, I got a Fort Bragg permit.

Having a car was not without problems. Everyone wanted to borrow it, and I had to say no. About 11:00 one night, the mean and often drunk sergeant in charge of our barracks awakened me and, in a stupor, demanded the use of my car. When I wouldn't give him the keys, he threw a tantrum. A fight seemed certain. With me at 5-foot-8-inches and he a 6-foot-plus cretin, I expected to be beaten to a pulp. Amazingly, he wheeled around and headed for his room where he tore his clothing to shreds.

Mostly, barracks life went along smoothly, especially considering that 30 or so men lived in one room, with each having no more turf than their cot and a foot locker plus 18 inches between beds.

About a third of the 66th General Hospital draftees were from the Finger Lakes district of central New York, towns like Geneva, Penn Yan, and Canandaigua. Dietz, who was, as the men said, "a card," was from Canandaigua. He had eyes of a woeful countenance that peered out of an appealingly cherubic face, all in all giving him the look of a lad a grandmother would love to hug. Just such a grandmother happened to be seated opposite him in the diner of a train that was taking him home for a short leave over the Thanksgiving weekend. Much taken by this nice-looking soldier, she asked him if he was was going home to see his family. Turning his sad eyes on her he said that yes he was, and what's more, to a mother who hadn't seen him for years. He weaved a sad tale to entertain the poor lady. Five years ago, he explained, he had run away from home to hide his shame over his youth of drunkenness and debauchery. Having sunk to the gutter, he woke up from a drunk one morning seeing the error of his ways. Determined to make a man of himself he quit drinking and joined the Army. Now, having rid himself of the demon rum, and with the help of the good Army food, he had regained his weight, and the bags under his eyes and the redness of his face were now gone. His tattered clothes had been replaced with an Army uniform which he was proud to wear. Perhaps by coming home he could help to restore the health of his poor mother who, he had learned from a soldier he had met from his hometown, had been pining away for him ever since he had left and was not expected to live many more months. How proud she would be of him. Of course the whole thing was a lie but totally believable from this quiet and innocent-looking young man. No doubt he had made the trip memorable for this sweet old lady.

Dietz and his buddy also would put on a wonderful act for new recruits. First, Dietz would ingratiate himself with them, helping them with things like stamping all their clothes with their Army serial numbers or showing them how to make their beds so tightly that a coin dropped on the top blanket would bounce, a test they would have to pass during inspection. Gradually, he let them in on a little of his life and his problem with his friend. The friend, he said, had entrusted him with his life savings, some $500, to bet with a bookie on number two in the third race at Saratoga. Number three had come in at 50 to 1 and now the men claimed he had picked number three. The friend thought Dietz pocketed the money . . . he would get Dietz; in fact, he had tried to kill him several times. If any of them saw the friend around, they should let him know so he could be on guard. His quiet manner and innocent-looking face made it all sound plausible. What kind of a brute would pick on such a nice guy?

With the build-up complete, Dietz and his pal, with a supporting cast who were in on the charade, would assemble on the barracks balcony where they would be seen by the new men coming from the mess. On signal, the two would start a cleverly rehearsed fight. At one moment, the pal would appear to have his fingers in Dietz's eyes about to gouge them out. In the next, Dietz would choke the man to the point where his breath would seem to be snuffed out. The grand finale came with Dietz hanging over the railing about to pass out from lack of air as his attacker had his two thumbs pressed against Dietz's windpipe. He seemed certain to fall to the concrete walk below at any moment. Of course the new men wanted to save their friend, but the old-timers (by about a month) would say, "Naw, let them have it out." The banter went back and forth as Dietz's chance for life waxed and waned. Then, with Dietz's last gasp, instead of falling, he suddenly recovered and the two put their arms around each other and walked happily away.

Social life on base consisted of drinking 3.2 beer on a Saturday night at the enlisted men's PX, a decrepit old wooden building down in a dell under the shade of giant willows. Supposedly 3.2 beer was sufficiently non-alcoholic to keep us from getting drunk, but with effort a soldier could get enough of it in him to have a good time. Old-timers had mastered the art of holding the neck of a beer bottle between their teeth, then tilting their head and opening their gullet, draining the entire bottle in one giant gulp. Many of the draftees were quickly learning the art. As the night wore on there were sure to be a few good fights, but they never got out of hand as the MPs were always nearby to break things up before anyone got hurt. Saturday night at the PX — soldiers, talk, singing, arguments, fights, being half drunk — there was no better life except being in the French Foreign Legion.

If some of my descriptions of Army life and its surroundings in 1941 seem unfamiliar to certain veterans, I would remind them that these scenes took place at the permanent part of an old military post where most of the soldiers were still old-timers of the Regular Army. The barracks were brick, very different from the two-story wooden barracks being thrown up in posts all over the United States to house civilians being drafted by the millions. On payday night, the rolling dice inside the wooden barracks in the new part made it sound like the barracks were being chewed to pieces by mice. Nary a sound could be heard outside our solid old concrete building, but the crap game inside was just as classy a social event.

The old post also had a very good movie theater. The first time I went, I was drawn to some good seats in the middle near the front by a nice-looking family that reminded me of my own. We were hardly seated when an MP told us to move. This was officers' turf. When I was a kid, my grandmother had an expensive Pierce-Arrow automobile. One of Buffalo's most fashionable department stores, Flint and Kent, featured a doorman to welcome the carriage trade. When we arrived in grandmother's limousine, he bowed like we were nobility. For Dad's Buick he forced a smile; and in my mother's Model T, he shooed us on, telling us to park around the corner. This was a man who could always recognize a car, but never a face. Now I was the Model T, second class even though I was serving my country, and I resented it. Yet, interestingly, at that time, had I been allowed to sit where I wanted, I wouldn't have seen anything wrong if colored men were restricted to the back rows of the theater.

It was hard getting used to saluting officers, but soon I would have a still harder time — I was getting saluted. When I left the OR wearing a surgeon's white gown, a cap, and a face mask that hung loose below my chin, I was taken to be a medical doctor and an officer. Enlisted men would snap to attention and give me a salute, which I would return with the sloppy salute in imitation of physicians who never learned to give a snappy salute. Had a soldier spotted my masquerade, he would have busted me one in the jaw. I also got salutes while driving my car, since such a luxury was assumed to be something only for officers. It certainly helped me live like them. On weekends off duty, I headed for resorts like Pinehurst or towns like Raleigh. The University of North Carolina at Chapel Hill was a favorite stop. Unlike most places that tolerated soldiers at best, students passing visiting soldiers gave friendly greetings. That felt good.

I originally had made up my mind to hate the Army, but it was getting harder and harder to do so.

On December 7th, 1941, the Japanese bombed Pearl Harbor. That meant goodbye to Captain Dear and the 66th General Hospital. We were soon on our way to Fort Dix to join a new hospital unit, the Harvard Medical Unit known as the 5th General Hospital. Captain Dear would be riding the trains again to pick out a new bunch of enlisted men to train in the operation of a General Hospital. Yet for all our gripes about him, there could be no complaints about the results. He had turned out a fine group of well-trained men.

In late December, we were given shots for yellow fever and typhus to immunize us for going overseas. By January, we were on our way to Fort Dix, teamed up with physicians and surgeons from the Harvard Medical School who had been called up when war began, every one of them a Thiessen. Even before we arrived at Fort Dix, preparations for going overseas were already under way, including plans to take along a grand piano the Harvard doctors had lined up. Goodbye to the clang of a broken-down upright piano in the 66th day room, hello Steinway and Chopin. We were going to be in a first-class outfit.

On the convoy across the Atlantic, I was to be the medic on a freighter, getting advice by radio from doctors who would be on the main troop ship, probably the *Normandie*, a French ship, the largest liner afloat and just about ready for service after being converted to a troop ship. Whether it was the *Normandie* I do not know, but when she caught fire and was destroyed at dock, plans for us shipping out were put on hold.

During the delay, I was loaned to a Fort Dix physician to help him vaccinate troops against typhus, smallpox, and other diseases, depending on where they were being sent. Among the doctors back at Fort Bragg, some were excellent and some were incompetent, but none were unprincipled. Here at Fort Dix, aside from the Harvard doctors who were revealing themselves to be as fine a group of men as I would ever know, I encountered physicians without principles. The doctor doing the vaccinating loaded multiple injections in a large syringe, then, without changing the needle, jabbed man after man who passed by in a line. I offered to get the sterilizer working, telling him I could change needles so fast he wouldn't be held up even a minute. But he ordered me to "keep my goddamn mouth shut." To my shame, like medical doctors who seldom blow the whistle on bad associates, I did as he said. I wonder how many cases of syphilis and other blood-transmitted diseases were passed on.

With our departure delayed, and more troops arriving for the next convoy, the Army had a situation on its hands like a hotel where one convention was still registered and another was arriving. Beds were double-decked and shoved so close together that we crawled in from the end to get in. The weather was bitter cold, and windows were kept closed; the air grew foul, and men got sick. My outfit was finally ready to pull out, but I was a patient in the hospital. Several Harvard physicians came to examine me to see what had happened to their scrub nurse. Through a fever, I heard one of them say, "Good God, they put him in a mental ward and he's got pneumonia." The doctors at Fort Dix had decided that I was feigning illness to get out of going overseas, and so . . . the mental ward. But it wasn't the first or the last time medics had jumped to the conclusion that a soldier faced with overseas service or combat had faked an illness. From their secure positions they couldn't imagine how loyalty to an outfit and comrades could outweigh fear. And I wasn't afraid; I was excited about going. Being the medical man aboard a freighter would have been a great experience, to say nothing about being stationed in England where my erstwhile outfit landed.

Being left behind, I had lost my friends. If I had been examined medically, instead of dealt with psychologically, with decent treatment perhaps I could have made the trip. Yet, as the future unfolded, I would get myself involved in an adventure many times more dangerous than a trip across the Atlantic.

Men released from jail, or from a hospital, having lost their outfit, were placed in a casual company for reassignment, in my case a casual company at Fort Dix. Delivered by ambulance, I was directed to a barracks. Inside about ten other casuals (that's what those of us without an outfit were called) were sitting around, mostly staring into space. A couple were playing cards. No one spoke to me. The atmosphere was sullen. Finding an empty bunk, I tossed down my gear and spoke to a soldier in the next bunk. He said hello then quickly turned his head, but not fast enough for me not to notice he had been crying. While unpacking, a sergeant I knew slightly back at Fort Bragg, one of the 66th's Regular Army cadre, appeared at my bedside. After helping me get settled, he suggested we go for a walk, someplace where we could talk without being heard. When we were out of earshot of others, he asked if I could type. I allowed that I could, but poorly. "No," he corrected, "you can type a hundred words a minute error-free." And he proceeded to advise me of the situation there. The first sergeant was a sadist who thought everyone there was a jailbird — scum — which gave him license to be cruel. According to the sergeant, he would even beat people.

The sergeant's information soon proved true. While typing away at my new job as temporary clerk in company headquarters, a casual came in to ask the first sergeant for a pass to visit his girlfriend in nearby Camden, whereupon the first sergeant, screaming and swearing, leaped up from his desk, grabbed the soldier by the collar, marched him to the door, and hit him in the face, sending him reeling over the entrance stoop and landing him on the ground, where he finished off the job with a swift kick to the soldier's groin. This all took place within sight of the company commander, a blue-eyed blond-haired prim cavalry officer about 25 who always carried a crop, although the Army no longer had horses. He was at his desk taking in the whole disgusting scene with a sheepish grin.

But back to my friend, the sergeant. He had said that every morning casuals were lined up like slaves. Commanding officers, mostly from infantry outfits looking for cannon fodder, went up and down the line inspecting the men and interviewing them for possible assignment in their outfits. If there was anything I did not want to be in the Army, it was an infantryman. The "slaves" were told to open their mouths for a look at their teeth; shirts were opened for a look at their build. Because the sergeant was the company clerk, he thought he might be able to get me assigned temporarily as a typist, which would get me out of the line-up for awhile. Then when an outfit came along with a good assignment, he would put me up for it.

Having been given the shaft by incompetent physicians who had put me in the mental ward, I felt no compunction about using family connections, and that night I called my father. Would he find out if the Fort Niagara hospital needed a surgical technician? Colonel Offinger, the commanding officer at Fort Niagara, was a friend of the family.

My transfer came through shortly, but before I left I got to know my friend from the 66th General a little better. Back at Fort Bragg he had been our supply sergeant and had impressed me as a cut above the average old Army non-coms. Here, seeing more of him, and becoming more and more impressed with his general knowledge and cultural interests, I couldn't resist asking him about himself. At first he ducked the question with a flip answer. Then finally he said, "Don't you know about me? I'm hooked on just about every drug there is." As a supply sergeant in a medical unit he could get all he wanted. My guess is that one of the Harvard physicians suspected the drug use and thus left him behind at Fort Dix.

Chapter 5

Full Circle

A T FORT NIAGARA, I met another first sergeant, Regular Army, 27 years old, who got where he was at such a young age because of his ability and his shrewdness. He had manipulated the colonel in charge of the hospital, a fat old doctor who let this first sergeant run things to the point where the colonel had no idea of what was going on. The colonel was in his pocket. The hospital had become the first sergeant's castle and he ruled it as such.

Five other officers — a physician, a surgeon, an anesthetist, and two nurses — completed the medical staff at Fort Niagara. The enlisted complement consisted of no more than 20, not much of a castle, but first sergeant was its king, a reign that remained unchallenged until the matter of the X-ray machine. It seemed the machine was on the list of the hospital's equipment, but it was shown to be missing during an Inspector General's audit. What kind of an organization was this that didn't take an inventory periodically? And would lose an X-ray machine? That's like losing an elevator in an apartment house. The poor old colonel was suspected of having sold it and pocketing the money. Naturally, he tried to shift the onus to his first sergeant.

As bad as it was for the first sergeant to have his reign under a cloud, insult was about to be added to injury. One April morning, Colonel Offinger, commanding officer of the entire post, had informed the man that I was coming up from Fort Dix to be assigned to the hospital's surgical staff. The source of power in an outfit decided who did what and where, power that the first sergeant had assumed, and power he needed to remain king of this castle. Furthermore, I would arrive with my own car. In short order I was in thick with the first sergeant's five best men, men who had been successful in civilian life — men with whom he would liked to have ingratiated himself.

In addition to me, three other men from this group were from Buffalo, where we went frequently, sometimes to be entertained in homes. I remember well the wonderful party given by one of the men's mother and father, warm Italian people who, anxious to know and welcome their son's friends, invited us to dinner in their large and impressive home in a section of Buffalo near the Niagara River favored by rich Italians. The woman, the epitome of an Italian mother, showed her affection for her son and her approval of his friends by stuffing us with delicious Italian food. Although the father stayed somewhat in the background, he was obviously proud of his son.

Our first sergeant probably had heard about the dinner and similar events and no doubt was jealous. I had usurped his friends and, worse, he hadn't selected me to be in his unit. Without his say, I had been forced on him by a colonel.

He found ways to vent his anger. Periodically, troops were instructed in the art of preventing venereal disease. With the entire company assembled, the first sergeant lectured on protection, including in his talk a display of condoms, soap for washing the groin, and a tube of argyrol, a thick brown silver-protein compound used prior to the discovery of antibiotics to control mucous-membrane infections. As a kid, at the first sign of a sore throat by any member of the family, my mother would head for the medicine cabinet and uncork the argyrol, load up a swab with the horrible stuff, line up the three of us kids and, despite our gagging and choking, paint the backs of our throats. It did nothing for us; a lot for her.

The first sergeant called me forward, positioning a chair to face the audience, then ordered me to serve as a part of his prevention demonstration. I certainly didn't like standing in front of a bunch of men with my genitals hanging out, and by the time he ordered me to demonstrate the application of the argyrol, I refused.

Normally the first sergeant wasn't stupid, but this time he was foolish enough to undermine his authority and embarrass himself by giving an order he couldn't enforce. I expected a summons to appear before a disciplinary board for disobeying an order, but it never came. What did come was a notice stating I had been reduced to a buck private and stripped of my technician's rating for "administrative reasons." At least he gave me credit for being the kind who wouldn't complain to my benefactor, Colonel Offinger, the post commander who could have raised hell over the whole incident.

Fort Bragg's post hospital had been virtually free of infections following operations. At Fort Niagara infection was routine. Suspecting the autoclave and other sterilizing equipment of not working properly, I sent samples off to a corps laboratory for testing, a routine procedure back at Fort Bragg and one I assumed was part of my job. As expected, the sterilizer was not operating properly. Corps inspectors came down hard on the hospital for letting equipment get in such bad shape. The colonel in charge of the hospital, however, was furious, saying I had made a fool of him, but that was not my intention. The first sergeant thought, I am sure, that this was my way of getting back at him.

By the summer of 1942, an epidemic of both scarlet fever and mumps broke out in the Army. Scarlet fever is known today as no more than a strep throat, but back then it was a nasty disease, often fatal. Mumps in adults, also dangerous as well as painful, could, in a serious case, render a man sterile. Fort Niagara's barracks were turned into hospitals as needed. I heard the Colonel tell the first sergeant to select medics to be ward orderlies who had already had both diseases and were therefore immune. Furthermore, to prevent the spread of the disease, orderlies were to be quarantined to the barracks until the epidemic was over. The first sergeant was immensely pleased to learn that I had had neither disease. Five men who had had both diseases and I ministered to the patients. Perhaps if I had gotten one or both of the diseases and almost died, the first sergeant might have felt he had his revenge, but despite confinement and close contact with sick men, I came through fine — except for looking pale, having spent four weeks never stepping outside the barracks.

Unfortunately, it looked like the game-playing between the first sergeant and me was going to continue. Worse, I was stuck in a minor job without chance of promotion, possibly for the duration of the war. Officers Candidate School, which I had applied for at Fort Bragg and from which I had heard nothing, was, I assumed, a missed opportunity. To apply again would have required a recommendation from the hospital commander, not a likely prospect without the support of his first sergeant. I might better have stayed at Fort Dix to have been picked up by some outfit where I could have served without prejudice and worked to win some sergeant stripes or a lieutenant's bar. I got what I deserved for using my father's influence.

Because I was stuck, Fort Niagara had a special appeal for me as a place to ride out the war in a kind of limbo. To be in that beautiful and historic place, to sneak away whenever possible for a view from the ramparts of the old fortifications to where the Niagara River flows into Lake Ontario, always helped me forget the day's problems and turn my mind to thinking about 18th-century soldiers stationed in this once-remote outpost of the New World. It didn't take much imagination to see French traders coming along the lake in the days when the French flag hung over the fort, or to shift the mind to the time of the American Revolution and see the British flag flying overhead. The history of the 18th-century wars that raged through this part of the world came alive for me. If I was to be stuck at Fort Niagara, and miss Hitler's war, I could at least perch on one of the old fort's ramparts and vicariously participate in wars past. Then, having absorbed all the history I could take sitting on the cold stone of a parapet, a few beers at a cozy saloon just outside the gate overlooking the Niagara River would seal the mood.

All the while, unknown to me, orders for me to attend an Officers Candidate program at the Army Medical Field Service School at Carlisle Barracks in Pennsylvania had been chasing me from Fort Bragg to

England, where I was supposed to be with the Harvard Group, then to Fort Dix where I had been a casual, and finally to Fort Niagara where the orders finally caught up with me.

On September 3, 1942, the Surgeon General promoted me to corporal and ordered me to attend a Medical Administrative Officers Candidate School at Carlisle Barracks. And things began to look up for the first sergeant as well. Not only was he rid of me, but the X-ray machine was found under a pile of coal in the hospital's basement.

Chapter 6

Tom Swift and
the Country Club

NOTHING IS classier, nothing demonstrates erudition more, than to recall a passage from literature to make a point, to express feelings. As I traveled toward Officers Candidate School, to help me with my feelings, my mind turned to the printed pages — not to Shakespeare or Milton or Frost, but to books in the Horatio Alger tradition. Good guy is put upon by bad guy; through thick and thin, good guy remains true. In the end, everything comes up roses. I recalled a series of novels featuring the indomitable Don Sturdy, an adventurer, and the indefatigable Tom Swift, a teenage inventor and racer of cars and motorcycles. Given fair play, there was no race. Tom Swift was just too swift; but alas, there were other ways to win — foul deeds. And there was always someone foul on the scene — a jealous competitor perhaps to loosen the bolts on Tom's motorcycle just as he was racing to the finish line. But alas, Tom's bike was equipped with pedals. Tom the wholesome pedaled the last hundred yards to victory. So it went in the lives of Don and Tom. And now in my life, the first sergeant's plan to take me down by quarantining me in a barracks where I was sure to succumb to mumps and scarlet fever had failed. In the tradition of the Sturdy and Swift novels, adversity turned to triumph. I was on my way to Officers Candidate School. I felt smug. My thoughts were mean and they were small. And they made me smile.

I threw myself into OCS like I was in a track meet. Grades were the goal. Other candidates were the competitors, many of whom had high IQs that should have given them an advantage. Halfway through the program, a quarter of the candidates had flunked out, surprisingly some of the brightest. A few stumbled when they couldn't stand in front of a platoon with a commanding presence and yell, "Forward march," a skill deemed essential for a Medical Administrative Officer. Otherwise, the bright ones should have shone. Often they didn't. Seemingly their education had let them down, their downfall relating to an inability to demonstrate abstract reasoning. I felt sorry for the fellow in the bunk next to mine, a bright guy, a nice guy. No one studied harder, no one memorized more facts. But the exams dealt more with applying principles, less with regurgitating facts. A test about sanitation raised the problem of an infantry on bivouac getting rid of fecal matter in frozen arctic soil. The instruction hadn't covered arctic conditions, but it did cover principles of sanitation. Either because he didn't understand the principles or couldn't apply them, he failed the exam. He was not alone. Further, as was true with so many of the military problems presented to the class, there was no right solution to the arctic problem. That threw them. As a college graduate with a liberal arts education, I was used to wrestling with problems beyond the range of $2 + 2 = 4$ — problems where there was no right answer, or no answer, only conjecture; the grade on the test depended on how well one summarized the evidence and displayed reasoning. In my answer I reviewed the principles of sanitation, then outlined a dilemma, finally providing what I acknowledged to be a not very satisfactory answer for a problem to which I could see no perfect solution.

Men tended to worry too much about answers without understanding the questions. A liberal education teaches that understanding the question is 9/10 of the answer. To study for an examination I concentrated on questions. What would I ask on a test were I the instructor? Applying this technique at Officers Candidate School, I hit the tests on the nose. When word got around that I could predict test questions, the men started to call me G-2, which stands for Intelligence — but not necessarily for smarts. G-2 is the designation for the officer in combat who asks the question, "What's the enemy going to do?" Then he tries to come up with the answer. My experience at Carlisle Barracks argues for a liberal arts education. It can give considerable leverage to an IQ. And like Tom Swift, I may have started out slowly, but I came in at the top of the class.

In any event, excelling in OCS called for excelling physically, mostly holding up during long marches. I was never any good in a sprint, but my father used to take long walks and I joined him whenever possible. Then in Ithaca, New York, where I went to college, where everything is on the side of the hill, my legs picked up strength. The Army never dished out anything I couldn't handle — hikes, patrols, or long marches. Returning dirty and tired after a 15-mile march, the last five filled with thoughts of getting into a hot shower, four other candidates and I, the top five in the class, were ordered to report, dirty and sweaty as we were, to the commanding general of the school. Appearing before him, wondering what we might have done wrong, he laid into us for our appearance, demanding to know what kind of soldiers we were, reporting to a general in our condition. Then he began to laugh, congratulating us on our achievements in school. Would we be interested in being assigned to a post in either San Francisco, Washington, D.C., or Denver? If so, we would have to graduate early. I chose to serve at a medical technicians school at Fitzsimmons General Hospital in Denver, Colorado. I liked to ski.

My presence in Denver wasn't so urgent that I couldn't take a few days en route for a stopover in Buffalo if I could get rail tickets from Buffalo to Denver via Chicago. No government bureaucracy ever achieved the arrogance of the Eastern railroads at the time. I waited in a long line for a ticket agent. The clock ticked, 10:30 a.m., 11:00, 11:55, at last only two customers ahead of me. Noon. The agent closed his window and took off for lunch. But the final insult was yet to come.

My train left for Chicago at 11:00 p.m. By 11:15, I was in my berth and sound asleep. How long after I do not know, but I was awakened when the train slammed to a halt. My head banged the end of my bunk. I thought that the brakes had been applied hard enough to lock for some reason. Somebody came into our car asking for a doctor, apparently having seen the caduceus on my uniform. But I hadn't awakened sufficiently to realize they might have been looking for me. In the morning I looked out the window and thought at first we were stopped outside Chicago, but then some of the scenery looked more like Angola, New York, which I recognized because my uncle lived nearby. Stretching my neck to see better out the window, I could see the cars ahead and the locomotive lying on their side in a ditch. The baggage car was split wide open. Trunks, suitcases, and boxes littered the area.

The first railroad agent to approach me was a lawyer with a waiver, which I signed, willingly giving up my right to sue. I wasn't injured. By plane I made it to Denver on time but without my foot locker, which had been in the baggage car. Fortunately it did not split open as so much of the luggage had. The railroad would ship it to me, but only if I paid for the freight. Years later, I traveled by rail behind the Iron Curtain in Hungary. There I found the railroad bureaucracy trying as hard as possible to be as arrogant and inefficient as ours, but they couldn't even come close.

❦

Fitzsimmons turned out to be more like a social club than an Army post. Colonel McCaw, Commandant of the Technicians School, was the president of the club, his wife the social chairman. Everyone affectionately called her Blaw, about as inappropriate a sobriquet as could possibly have been attached to this lively little 5-foot, 101 pounds of fun with sparkling eyes. Most of the social events took place at the McCaw home right on the post, although sometimes we partied at the Officers Club just down the street. The very day I arrived at Fitzsimmons, Blaw invited me — or should I say summoned me? — to their home. All the members were there — colonels, majors, captains, and lieutenants. This was the first of many such parties. The big cheese, the general in overall command of both the hospital and the school, attended only one party during my stay at Fitzsimmons. At that party Blaw asked me to help serve the drinks. I had a tray full of them, when somebody bumped me. The load landed in the general's lap.

I had arrived at the door of the McCaws' that first night with my brass shined and my fly double-checked, still thinking of myself as an enlisted man, not sure of what to expect at an officer's party. Colonel McCaw met me at the door with his hand extended, solving the problem of whether or not I should salute. With the same pleasant grin that greeted me earlier in his office, he welcomed me to his home. Blaw descended on me, as she did to all the guests, then after a most warm welcome, she directed me to the bar to help myself. The selection consisted of bourbon, ice, and water. It was bourbon or nothing, so I drank bourbon.

Never before or since have I ever been to a party as a stranger where I immediately felt so comfortable. I was talking to everybody. I had another drink; the room spun a quarter turn. Bourbon was strong stuff. I knew that the first night in the Colonel's home was no time to make a fool of myself. Our Catholic chaplain looked like the room was spinning for him as well. His thick black Irish hair, neatly combed when he had arrived at the party, was hanging over his forehead. Later, on other occasions — parties at the McCaws', or the Officers Club, or on the many forays to the bars in downtown Denver — when I saw his hair beginning to hang loose, I knew he was getting looped. I knew there would be no morning mass unless I went to his room and dragged him out of bed, which, being a serious Catholic at the time, I did. The chaplain was just a young priest — handsome, and a great guy — but not strong enough to resist the temptation to sin, an opportunity never offered to him before joining the Army. I hoped the Colonel would notice what was going on and get the chaplain transferred to some field outfit where there wouldn't be so many opportunities to party. Sober, he was a marvelous chaplain.

After my own bourbon spin, however, I held, rather than drank, my drink. Blaw, seated in a comfortable chair surrounded by young officers, beckoned to me, taking my hand with a slight pressure to guide me to the chair next to her being vacated by a captain who sensed it was time to depart. Where was I from? Had I been to college? What did I do after

Second Lieutenant John L. Munschauer, Medical Administrative Corps.

college? Did I have brothers or sisters? Lots of questions. But they came through as friendly interest rather than the "third degree."

Blaw made me feel that she would have liked to talk to me all evening, but she had to greet new guests. "Would you," she asked, "go in the kitchen and see if the peas are boiling? If they are, turn them

Fitzsimmons, 1943 — one of the Colonel's daughters is married.

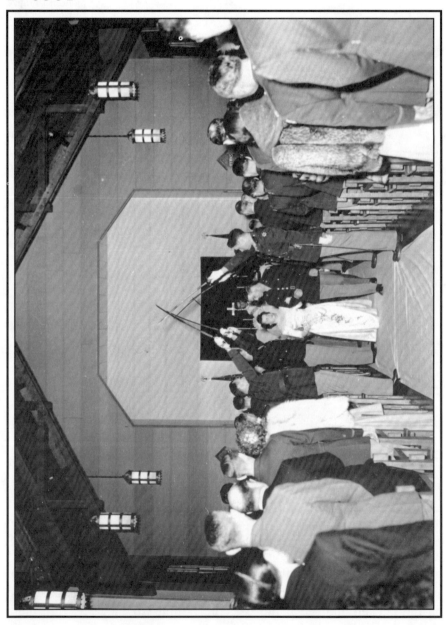

down." In the kitchen I met Anne, a beautiful girl about 20, the McCaws' youngest daughter. I did such a great job of turning down the peas that I was sent into the kitchen several more times. Potatoes had to be mashed, a steak had to be cut in thin slices, food had to be put in serving dishes and carried to the dining room. Each time I went into the kitchen, I met another of the McCaw daughters. With them more or less in charge of the kitchen, and with Blaw in her chair enjoying her company while at the same time giving orders to me and the other young officers, the dinner seemed to appear without any fuss on the part of the host and hostess. Feeling useful and having the host and hostess so relaxed made the evening fun. I knew I had made it into Blaw's club.

We young officers were being checked out. After all, we might become prospects for the McCaw daughters, but it wasn't just that. Blaw liked us. Even when we didn't prove to be likely candidates, we were still invited. With no plans to become a doctor or a lawyer after the war, just some vague ideas about going into business, Blaw considered my prospects for making a living shaky. I probably checked out as only a seven on her scale of ten. Potential sons-in-law headed for one of the professions were a better bet. The eldest daughter was already married to a dentist, and another dentist seemed to be scoring points with the second in line, which pleased the McCaws. The couple was married, the wedding performed with all the pomp and circumstance of a military ball — a grand affair. That left Anne to be pursued by a more suitable candidate. But I spent a lot of time at the McCaws and watched Anne play the field, which was an education for me as I had no sisters.

On duty, the Colonel remained aloof. In the tradition of the Regular Army, he had an old-time Regular Army sergeant to deal with the likes of us junior officers, except his sergeant had been commissioned a major when we had entered the war. The major, rigid in mind and body, sat in the outer office from Colonel McCaw with his perfectly groomed gray hair and a mustache, and his immaculately pressed uniform decorated with three rows of colored ribbons indicating years of service in many parts of the world. He looked like and was a man not to be trifled with. Reporting to him was as strict a military affair as reporting to General Patton, the disciplinarian terror who demanded that even combat soldiers keep their shoes shined and their buttons polished. With the major, our uniforms had to be perfect, our hair cut short, and we had better state our business succinctly. But we liked him. He was fair. Yet he never became a member of the McCaw club.

If you are reading beneath my praise of the major a suspicion that I still had a chip on my shoulder when it came to Regulars, you have it right. Herman Wouk probably had a similar one on his shoulder, then knocked it off in *The Caine Mutiny,* a story about a Navy Regular who got pushed up the ladder to a job he couldn't handle. After ripping the man apart, Wouk turned around and pointed out that these Regulars, despite the country's disdain, held the military together while the nation neglected it, giving the country some semblance of a force to defend against Hitler and Japanese Prime Minister Tojo. For this we should be grateful. Colonel Arndt Mueller, a man who produced one of the finest fighting units in the entire Army, the 3rd Battalion of the 63rd Infantry, helped to put the matter in better perspective with his unstinting praise for the old-time Regulars who helped him train an Infantry company of civilian soldiers when he was a company commander at Fort Leonard Wood just before the war. He liked the old-timers and he enjoyed telling about them.

As the story goes, one day while walking past the barracks housing the 3rd Platoon of Company K, Mueller heard a voice inside. He recognized it as one of his Regulars, a sergeant, orienting recruits. "At ease, men. In case you missed it, you're in K Company, Third Battalion, Sixty-Third Infantry of the Sixth Division — the best goddamned company in the Army. This is the Third Platoon; the best damned platoon in the Army. I am your platoon sergeant, Norwood G. — and the 'G' stands for God! That's what I am as far as you're concerned. You got any problems, suggestions, come to me. If I don't have answers, there is your company commander, Lieutenant Mueller, who is a hard case. Remember his name because he gets very upset if you don't recognize him. He won't get on your ass. No, he'll get on my ass and that makes me very unhappy. The company commander got himself an old-timer for a first sergeant named Terpstra who is the meanest sonofabitch next to me. Don't cross these two up because if you do, that will be the sorriest day of your life." It was pure bull, but this mixed with a basic fairness set the stage for turning butchers, bakers, and candlestick-makers into first-class soldiers.

My duties at the Fitzsimmons School were somewhat like that of a homeroom teacher. Administratively the trainees were in my charge. For instruction they spent most of the day in class, some to become dental technologists, others X-ray technicians, still others to take courses in lab technology, so I didn't need a platoon sergeant like "Norwood G." to train the men. My job as one of several company commanders was to house them, get them to clean their barracks, lead them in calisthenics, take them on hikes to keep them fit, get them paid, discipline them if they acted up, and upon graduation see that they were shipped off to hospitals where they were needed. In all such matters, when I had to deal with higher authority, I saw the major. If I had been a medical instructor concerned with teaching and curriculum, Colonel McCaw would have been the person to consult.

After a year of "homeroom" duties, I got a different assignment, this one even less demanding, and one involving men so smart and well behaved they didn't even need me, much less a sergeant. The Army, seeing the need to keep a flow of men going to medical school, yet not wanting to let them get off the hook for military service, solved the problem by enlisting medical students and sending them to medical school. My brother earned his MD as a private soldier, his tuition paid by the Army. Frequently, the time between enlistment and the beginning of school was a matter of months. Fitzsimmons formed a company to warehouse these men until school opened. I was appointed commanding officer of the warehouse.

These future doctors became the most physically fit men in the Army. There wasn't much to do except run them through close-order drill, give them calisthenics, and, because I liked to look at cattle, hike the countryside from one Aberdeen Angus ranch to another. When not hiking, I showed them Army training films, becoming particularly interested in those about infantry tactics. I began to get hooked on the art of warfare and tactics, subscribing to the *Infantry Journal* and the *Command and General Staff Journal.* Like a celibate monk in a monastery who only loses his virginity vicariously through reading, I had my films and journals to indulge my fascination for war.

Life in Denver was good. All that was needed was a car to get to the mountains to ski. Al Pagano, another skier, saw an ad in the *Rocky Mountain News* for a 1934 Dodge for $125. Except for rust that could be painted over, it looked OK. Al asked if we could share the cost, but he

The
$100
1934
Dodge
ski
car.

wanted to get the price down. He faced off to bargain with the owner; Al aimed for $75, the owner for $125. Going at it nose to nose, each head shaking back and forth as they argued, the bargaining heated up. If their heads — and noses — had hit, it would have been like two baseball bats colliding, and shattering. Suddenly, the owner said, "OK, $100." Al said, "OK." The man shrieked in glee, "I would'a sold it for $75!" Al yelled back: "I said I would have paid $125!" "Yike," the owner wailed.

We picked up the car the next day and drove it home, to discover the hubcaps were missing. Al cursed the owner, insisting we go back for them, but I said even he wouldn't be that cheap, to keep the hubcaps. Besides, what would anyone do with old 1934 Dodge hubcaps? We went back, and the man gave them up without any embarrassment, saying he meant to clean them for us, then forgot.

That old Dodge never once let us down in our mountain adventures, although every 20 minutes on steep grades, just like Old Faithful in Yellowstone Park, she would spew water and steam from the radiator, covering the windshield with rusty grime. Buying the Dodge was the most exciting thing that happened to me at Fitzsimmons.

Eventually Colonel McCaw was transferred to Alaska — finally a chance to get someplace interesting during the war. He promised to get me transferred there as a member of his new command, but after a while it became apparent it wasn't going to happen. There was nothing to do except relax and enjoy the good life at Fitzsimmons.

One of Our Menaces
Ho hum, ho hum
I've a happy life,
A nice little wife;
I've a little money
From a nice little store;
Ho hum, ho hum,
I wish there was a war.

Life is very pleasant
And always just the same;
I can call the mayor
By his first name;

As a golf-player
I've a low score;
Ho hum, ho hum,
I wish there was a war.

My wife gives a party,
It's really very nice,
We have a little salad,
Coffee and ice;
I sing a funny ballad,
The folks yell for more —
Ho hum, ho hum,
I wish there was a war.

I'd like to loot cathedrals
And hang men from trees,
I'd like to have a try at
A few atrocities;
I'd like a world-wide riot,
I don't care what it's for —
Ho hum, ho hum,
Let's have a war.

(Reprinted by permission of The Putnam Publishing Group from
SPILT MILK by Morris Bishop. Copyright © 1942 by Morris
Bishop. Renewed © 1970 by Morris Bishop.)

Part Two

Bayonet

Chapter 7

The Beat of the Drum

ON Sunday, December 7, 1941, just as they had done every Sunday after mess, a disgruntled PFC and a corporal made their way to the day room of the 66th General Hospital. I was already there, plopped in a wonderfully comfortable old Morris chair reading a tattered 1939 issue of *Life*. Entering and seeing me, they headed for the pool table, selected cues, chalked the tips, and began playing without saying a word. There was talk they were fairies, and some jerk had peed in the PFC's bay rum aftershave. Draftees were getting the blame, and I was a draftee. But even without this insult, these two wouldn't have been friendly. They were Army Regulars, men who enlisted as unemployed refugees of the Great Depression. This day room, this old brick barracks at Fort Bragg, this was their turf, their home, and we new guys were taking over. They made us feel about as welcome as a sheriff with an eviction notice.

We would have been glad to let them have the day room, the barracks, all of Fort Bragg, the nearby city of Fayetteville, the whole damned Army. We were counting the days, hours, and minutes to when we could return home. Home for them was the Army. In it they experienced life in a kind of limbo revolving around playing pool, drinking beer, and going into town to do some knocking around — or knocking up. I had come into the day room to wait for friends who were going into town with me to knock around.

The PFC had just finished a shot when another Regular bounded into the room, headed for the corner to an old upright piano, seated himself before the keyboard, flexed his fingers like a concert pianist loosening up, then began playing "Meloncoxy Baby," as he called it, one of the two tunes in his repertoire. Following that he switched to the second, "Fliver LaSalle," then back to "Meloncoxy Baby," and so on. A peculiar kind of a guy, he could hear a tune and play it, but only these two tunes stuck with him — and drove everyone else nuts as he played them over and over. After one of his "concerts" I remarked that he would make an interesting psychological study. "Geez," he said overhearing me, "you sure know big words."

The PFC and the corporal, already in a bad mood, managed to ignore the playing until the third rendition of "Meloncoxy Baby," then their game began to go downhill. By the fourth, the PFC, now missing easy shots, snapped on the radio and turned up the volume. Out wailed a hillbilly in a lugubrious rendition of "You Are My Sunshine, My Only Sunshine." Without missing a beat, our pianist switched to trying to play along. The PFC, quick to lose his temper and already in trouble after a fight at the Post Exchange, reddened; his lips moved silently as he counted to ten. The rendition was too much for me. I got up to leave, when the radio cut to an announcer. The Japanese had bombed Pearl Harbor. The PFC listened for a moment, then finished his shot. The corporal took up his cue, then put it down and went over and turned off the radio. Their game went on, not a word said. The pianist slid back to "Meloncoxy Baby." I started to say something, but got a look that told me to drop it.

Pearl Harbor was not the only momentous event that I was to see met with indifference. In the Philippines in 1945, my platoon had been fighting in the hills. We had taken one, but more were ahead. A news sheet from battalion headquarters arrived to be passed around. The war in Europe was over! Each guy read it and passed it on without saying anything. That war was as remote to us as the First World War. Finally, one guy said something that covered it all: "Who gives a shit? What I want to know is, what about the next hill?"

Looking back, had anyone told me I would be leading an Infantry platoon in those hills, I would have told them they were off their rocker. I who was drafted kicking and screaming; I who reacted to Pearl Harbor by being thankful I was safely in the medics; I who got the best deal imagined when I was commissioned a Medical Administrative Officer and stationed in Denver; I who found a home at the Colonel's home enjoying his bourbon and the company of his daughters; I the timid when it came to adventure — I was on those hills in the Philippines because I volunteered for the Infantry.

A war was going on. I was in the Army, but I wasn't in the war. Soldiers were showing up on the streets wearing "fruit salad" — colored bars pinned over their left pockets to indicate campaigns, one with red and blue stripes on yellow for service in the Pacific Theater, others for campaigns in Africa, Italy, and Europe. Colors varied according to the medal — purple for those who had been wounded, red for the bronze star, and so on for the silver star, and others. In almost four years of service I was entitled to wear a yellow ribbon for good conduct as an enlisted man. Whoopee! Just the medal for me to wear, since one of my duties was to give a pep talk to enlisted men to get them to volunteer for the Infantry. The medal I should have been given was for those talks. I did such a good job, I signed up myself.

Why would anyone do anything so stupid? Back in 1936 when I was a freshman at Cornell in Ithaca, Emil Kohm, a tailor and the town's leading cracker-barrel philosopher, predicted I would do just such a thing. I thought him mad on two counts. A war? Where did he get such a crazy notion? And me signing up? He didn't know us Munschauers. We're timid. But let me tell you about Emil. People passing his shop on State Street could look into his storefront window and see him sitting cross-legged on a table cutting and sewing, one eye on the cloth, the other looking out the window for someone he might know to hail in. He knew me because he made my father's suits.

On one of my frequent trips downtown from the campus to buy ciga- rettes — a local drugstore sold them for $1.10 a carton and I'd buy them to sell for $2.50 in my fraternity — Emil beckoned me in as I passed by. He had just been to Canada for its greatest tourist attraction of the '30s, the Dionne Quintuplets. Their multiple births, unheard of before the days of fertility pills, caused a sensation — and a chance for the enter- prising Dr. Dafoe, who delivered the quints, to make a bundle. Under Dafoe's sponsorship a nursery was built with one-way windows where the curious, for a fee, could observe the quints getting fed, diapered, burped, and put down to sleep. Emil wanted me to have a stone from the Dionne driveway, predicting that my life would be blessed with many children. Had I known that I was to marry three times, each time adding more members to my family, everything from kids to adults with kids, until I became the patriarch of a 42-person extended family, I would have dropped the stone then and there and run from his store. And given his war prediction, I would have kept running until I was beyond the city limits of Ithaca.

Finishing with the Dionnes, he turned to Hitler and Mussolini, men he took seriously. How could he? They were clowns. We saw them in action in the newsreels shown in the movie theaters, our equivalent of TV news. Their ranting and raving was a joke. All anyone had to do to be a comic at a party was to mimic Hitler or Mussolini, especially Mussolini. And to us the Japs were just a bunch of vandals savaging remote Manchuria; tragic but no concern of ours. "Nevermind," Emil said, "war is coming. And just as in the World War when students paraded behind a band all the way down State Street to the recruiting office like children following the Pied Piper, so will you join the parade when war comes. I pray you won't, but you will."

I laughed. Hitler had a tiny following in the United States, including a few influential people who assured us that he was a good guy. Although we could see ominous clouds on the horizon, we were all too ready to listen to anyone who claimed to see a silver lining in those clouds. And the word Nazi didn't mean what it does today. Many people who were anything but sympathetic to Nazi politics felt Hitler's eco- nomics had merit. The world was suffering from economic stagnation.

Rising tariffs in every country were choking off trade. Germany had been sinking under the weight of reparations demanded by the Allies after the First World War, pulling down other countries with her. When Hitler came along, Germany began to prosper. Some saw this as the sign of a man who could raise enough hell to shake some economic sense into world leaders.

Few understood what Hitler had in mind for the Jews, and what little was known about German anti-Semitism didn't necessarily turn people off. Anti-Semitism was not unusual in the United States in the '30s. My conscience is scarred. Many of the students I especially liked in college were Jewish, yet, like my fraternity brothers at Delta Phi, I would never have considered pledging a Jew.

Easing my conscience somewhat is my memory of a party when I was about 16. Some guy launched into an anti-Semitic tirade. The more he ranted the more I thought him a fool. I found myself blurting, "I'm a Jew." I am not, but at that moment I wanted to see him squirm. What if I had been a German and a student in Munich during the '30s? What if a band came marching down the street? Would I have stood up and said, "I am a Jew?" Or would I have been out front swaggering? Or a hang-dog in the back of the pack, a coward afraid of what might happen if I didn't go along with the crowd? As we condemn the Germans, we should ask, what would we have done?

Until President Ronald Reagan agreed to go to a cemetery at Bitburg, Germany, to lay a wreath at a memorial for German soldiers, he was considered the "Teflon president" who could commit gaffes and never get stuck with the consequences. He could not, however, shake the outrage of the American Jews over his going to Bitburg to commemorate a place where SS troops were buried. Was it justified? Who knows? He never had a chance to speak his mind. What if he had stood over those graves to ask that we Americans consider what we might do if someday we were caught up in the tide of history like that which had ensnared the Germans? What if Reagan had warned us to beware of the kind of demagoguery that led so many to their graves? What if he had warned us to be wary of letting conditions develop that would warp our minds and trap us into behaving like barbarians? Had Reagan so spoken, would the righteous among us have been so sanctimonious? When we decide that certain ideas are right and certain ideas are wrong, we are quick to shout down those who do not agree with us. I have spent my working life in a college community where students are supposed to learn critical listening, but there is little listening here. There is shouting here. We should learn from Hitler: first we shout, next we shoot.

One doesn't just see a parade and jump into it. Parades don't form overnight. They are orchestrated. When we were at peace and I got trapped by Roosevelt's military draft, I felt I was part of his orchestration to get us into a war that was none of our business. Before the radio announcement of the bombing at Pearl Harbor, I resented wearing a uniform; after the announcement, I returned to my barracks to shine my shoes and polish my brass. Like a switch turning on a light, attitudes changed. And we had a parade, a cavalcade. I was ready to march, especially carrying the banner of a medical technician where there was little chance of getting shot.

Today the Hitler war is known as the good war, but most of us who fought didn't join the parade waving the flag because we thought it a noble cause. We followed no Pied Piper's slogan about making the world safe for men and women of all religions and all races. The Japanese dropped bombs that ignited Pearl Harbor, and we were mad. We were threatened. We were scared. We always had a subconscious fear of the yellow races, and now that fear was real. Pearl Harbor ignited emotions. Then the Germans joined in and threw gasoline on the fire. Once lit, revenge, hatred, patriotic fervor, heroics, and greed fueled the fire, and it wasn't going to stop until one side or the other was burned out. Only now can we say we fought because we were dedicated to the ideal of humanity, an ideal we discovered mostly by poking through the ashes and discovering the Holocaust.

Seldom did we catch a glimpse of what we were fighting for other than revenge and self-interest, and when we did, it didn't sink in. What we saw in newsreels or read in the papers about German or Japanese subjugation of others did give us some idea that civilization itself was at stake, but not until a minor thing happened one afternoon at Fitzsimmons in Denver did the real meaning of the war hit me. I had had enough of working away at my desk in company headquarters. It was hot and I went outside for a breath of fresh air. Some soldiers were standing around talking about the war. Americans had landed in Italy and things seemed to be looking up. The first sergeant of the company, a German-

Jewish refugee, an intellectual and cultured gentleman, and I suspect wealthy before Hitler confiscated his fortune, came out to ask me a question. One of the soldiers, knowing he was Jewish, asked, "Sarge, when we win the war will you go back to Germany and claim your property?" He didn't answer at first, just looked at the soldier, just looked at me. His eyes transferred a message to me that I can't explain, a message of terror perhaps. He seemed to be holding back tears. Very slowly, very sadly, he said, "You don't have the vaguest idea of what is going on in Germany, do you?" I didn't. Who did? But from his manner we knew the war meant far more than things material.

America was naive. The idea of genocide was beyond belief. The story of the Holocaust wasn't known, or at least not believed until after the war. Even now it is hard to take in. But had we really understood the Holocaust, would that have sent us rushing to join a parade to the recruiting office? Did Japan's rape of China and Manchuria quicken our pace? Do high-minded thoughts about the human condition start the foot tapping to the beat of a drum? Or is it something more primordial? Deep down, is it the "I'd like to loot cathedrals and hang men from trees, I'd like to have a try at a few atrocities"?

Many years later, when my daughter's seventh-grade teacher said that I must have been a barbarian because I fought in a war, he didn't have it right. The verse did not fit any of the soldiers with whom I fought. Undoubtedly it fit some elsewhere. With millions in the Army, there were bound to be some rotten apples. I confess that it bothers me that I did such a crazy thing as to leave the medics for the Infantry, and I often think "Why?" In my work as a career counselor I learned that to know the man, know the boy.

Men, when they are boys, get tuned to a beat. When I was a kid we didn't have television but we did have Grosset and Dunlap, and other publishing firms that ground out cheap novels. I couldn't wait for each new edition of the *Boy Allies*, a series of novels about soldiers in the First World War whose heroic activities had more to do with winning the war than the efforts of General Pershing. The stories are long forgotten, but they planted the seed of a notion that there was something fine and heroic in being a soldier. It grew like a virus; it altered something in my personality that would subconsciously start my foot tapping to the beat of war drums. In my teens I read more sophisticated books about wars.

Kenneth Roberts had me marching with the rabble in arms in his novels about the French and Indian War and the Revolution. (But good God, if my propensities were implanted during my formative years from reading, I hope the same doesn't hold for my grandchildren from watching television. I hate to think of them being transmogrified into little monsters.)

The beat of the drum from my childhood was reawakened by Ernie Pyle's newspaper columns eulogizing the common soldier and by Bill Mauldin's poignant cartoons of combat soldiers. Reading about what men were going through in Europe and Japan made me feel ashamed of my comfortable life in Denver. By the time I was assigned the Pied Piper's role to lure men into the Infantry I could orchestrate the message with fervor because I was devoted to the music. The uniform I longed to wear was not decorated with aviator's wings, glamorous as they were, nor one featuring a caduceus like mine; it was the uniform displaying a Combat Infantry Badge pinned over the left breast. For all the millions of men in the Army and the Navy, it was that thin line of infantrymen at the front who were taking the territory that would win the war. All the others were just support.

But, only hero worship fit my temperament, not heroism. I could admire heroes in the Infantry, not join them. That being the case, I might as well stop daydreaming and enjoy my life.

> Life was very pleasant
> And always just the same;
> I could call the Colonel
> By his first name.
> Ho hum, ho hum,
> Deep inside of me
> I wished I was in the war.

Beware of the bored man. Beware of the man whose life is a vacuum. Nature demands it be filled. Hitler's parade sucked in Germans by the millions. Drug dealers' best customers are those who need to fill a void in their lives (climbing Mount Everest is a better way to do it). While life in Denver was pleasant, it was just vacuous enough to trouble me. The books I read, the speeches I gave exhorting others to join the parade, the medals I wanted to wear on my jacket, the adventure I sought kept my foot tapping to the beat of the drum, but it would take a shove to get me into a parade.

Howard Hufford, a lively young lieutenant and a great friend, gave the shove. No need to detail the vacuum left in his life by telling about the failure of a love that didn't turn into a friendship, or his boredom with his duties as Medical Administrative Officer. He was vulnerable. He was the kind of guy to climb Mount Everest. I should not have fed him my Infantry propaganda. He got excited, then he excited me with his excitement. The first thing we knew we were in the parade.

But Howard took just a few steps before his mother, a woman to be reckoned with, the widow of a Regular Army officer, pulled some strings to bring her son back in line. The War Department informed him that it would be against the Geneva Convention for a medical man to bear arms, and so his transfer to the Infantry was rescinded. Sick to my stomach at my own hasty decision, I thought perhaps a little string-pulling on my behalf might be a good idea. But to renege on this decision to participate in the action would mean missing out on the greatest event of the century, and deep down that was the strongest pull. I did not want to miss the show. The stories of adventure from my childhood reading were poking at me from somewhere back in the recesses of my brain. I am a romantic. Romantics do stupid things. I stuck with my decision.

In short order I was off to the Infantry School to be converted to an Infantry platoon leader. Then for a while it looked like my bold move to see the war wasn't going to work and I was again going to watch the war from an Army post in the United States. From the Infantry School I went to Fort McClellan, Alabama, to train second-generation Japanese Americans, known as Nisei. No officer had it easier. These men would do whatever they were asked to do without question. When holding a rifle to shoot, we taught them to place the butt of the gun against their shoulder, their left arm underneath to steady it, the right arm arched over it, which didn't seem to make sense. The typical American always asked why. Only after being shown how the upper arm acted like an arch in a bridge that gave strength would they do it. The Nisei asked no questions, raised no objections; they just did as directed. And more. In the barracks on their free time, manual in hand, they studied the proper position, coached each other, and practiced and practiced to get it right.

They tried to teach me a little Japanese, but, as my three-year-old granddaughter said when she couldn't pronounce a word, it wasn't "comfortable" to my tongue. When we were out on the parade ground, however, and my men got mixed in with the others during a break, instead of having to run around like the other officers shouting in English for men to assemble, I learned to yell something like *"Koko nee, atsumari,"* meaning very roughly, "Here I am, come here." This turned out to be a very effective way to get heard, but these were the most useless words I could possibly have learned, as I was soon on my way to fight the Japanese and I certainly didn't want to shout to them, "Here I am, come here!"

At the time, however, it looked like I might be shouting *"Koko nee, atsumari"* until the end of the war. I had graduated from the Infantry School at Fort Benning in November of 1944 and it was getting on into December, with every indication that I had landed a permanent assignment as a training officer. Such was my lot in the Army, to be in training or training.

Chapter 8

Romance and the Legend

O N JANUARY 19, 1945, the romance and excitement
I sought began in San Francisco aboard the *General
Langfit*, a 13,000-gross-ton troop ship based on the
design of a C4 tanker hull. The ship rated at 17 knots — we
were told we were going 22, but friends who know ships
doubted it — fast enough to outrun submarines and cross the
South Pacific without destroyer escorts. At any time, peace or
war, there is nothing quite like being on ship as she casts
off, but add to that dangerous waters and destinations
unknown, and that's the stuff for romantics. One by one lines
were cast off. The ship began to vibrate. Water churned and
foamed between ship and pier. One foot, two feet, three feet,
slowly, ever so slowly, we were edging from the pier. We were
under way. We passed beneath the Golden Gate Bridge. To

where? To death? That's the possibility that puts the crown on high adventure.

Land left behind, the *Langfit* headed into the Pacific ground swells, ocean waters moving east that hit the California coast and bounce like an echo, sending mounds of water back out to sea that slowly rolled the *Langfit* to starboard, then to port; back and forth, back and forth, slowly, slowly, back and forth, inexorably back and forth. None on board, not even the most seasoned sailors, could escape feeling sick. Remedies for seasickness are as many as those for poison ivy and equally useless, but I followed the advice to keep eating and kept down what I ate — barely. In the hold, 2,807 enlisted men were bunked on canvas cots stacked three high. Men in the top bunks were sick. And the law of gravity hadn't been repealed. Men in the middle bunks were sick. And again the law of gravity continued to operate. Men in the lower bunks were sick. All I have to do is remember the scene and I may be sick.

Necessarily, the military is autocratic, not democratic, yet even when that is understood, civilians in uniform who have been reared to believe that all men are created equal cannot easily put aside the notion of equality, especially on a Navy ship, where inequality is flaunted. Enlisted men *ate*; officers *dined* — on fine china served by colored men dressed like waiters in a five-star restaurant. Coffee was poured from silver urns. The china and silver was an extravagance, the service an embarrassment. While enlisted men slept on bunks in the bowels of the ship, officers slept on beds in staterooms, albeit double-decked for the Army officers who were passengers. But the comfort of a bed was short-lived. The closer to the equator we got, the hotter we got, the more we sweated, the more the sheets, mattress pads, and mattresses soaked in the sweat. The sweat began to ferment and to stink, to a sickly sweet stink. Perhaps the Navy officers' sheets got changed; ours were not. Down in the hold, men sweated as much, and probably more, but their canvas cots helped to evaporate the sweat, lessening the stink. For once, the enlisted men got the better of it. Years later, while driving across a bridge over Chesapeake Bay, I spotted a ship built on a C4 tanker hull. I looked closer. I almost drove off the bridge. It was the *Langfit*! I knew. I could smell her.

For 30 days the *Langfit* was our world, 30 days of hanging around on deck enjoying the sun, 30 days of staring at the sea and the sky, 30 days of meeting people we wish we could meet again, 30 days of wonderful reading, often two books a day in my case, thanks to the ship's library of Armed Forces paperbacks. Paperbacks are common today, but these were the first I had seen.

For 30 days our stateroom became a gambling den organized by my bunkmates. The stakes got high. Winnings and losses mounted. Things got nasty. I stayed out of it. Sergeant Soileau, the mess sergeant in an outfit I would eventually join and a former professional gambler, filled me in on what happened. He said there may have been someone in the game who was a professional and cheating. It wasn't unusual to find a man who can deal any kind of hand he wants. But it wasn't very smart of him because someone would smell a rat. A troop ship was the ideal place for a professional. Every player has a streak of luck, sometimes good, sometimes bad. All that is needed to win is the capital to ride out streaks of bad luck. Most men won't be able to do this; a professional will. With staying power, a pro will gradually clean up. I suspect that when Soileau, who refused to gamble with friends, got on a ship to go home after the war, he had plenty of money available to do a little cleaning up himself.

While my bunkmates gambled in the stinking stateroom, I would be out on deck tucked behind a ventilating shaft or hidden under a life boat so that the men lounging around on deck wouldn't see me doubled in laughter reading some zany author like Thorne Smith. I read trash; I read the classics. In a letter to my mother I mentioned reading and much disliking Samuel Butler's *The Way of All Flesh*, a book I read again at age 60 and loved. It's the story of a young man struggling unsuccessfully to make his way in life. Back then, I thought the hero was just a jerk who couldn't shed a lot of baggage from his childhood. Years later, as a career counselor dealing with people who couldn't shake loose from their backgrounds, I found the book to be poignant as well as enjoyable.

At 17 knots, the *Langfit* was fast enough to get us to Hollandia, New Guinea, without a naval escort. There, at anchor, we sat for days. Or was it weeks? Already I was beginning to lose my sense of time. When off to war it is better that the mind remains suspended, looking neither forward nor back. We lay at anchor not more than a hundred yards from land, never getting a chance to go ashore. We hung over the rail watching an endless parade of trucks and jeeps going back and forth, presumably doing something. Rumor had it that General MacArthur, a hero on the home front but an imperious sonofabitch to soldiers, had built himself some kind of castle in the hills over the harbor. Some said they saw it, pointing to what looked to me like an outcropping of rocks high on a hill.

The best show was watching the comings and goings in and around the harbor. Troop ships, tankers, freighters, landing craft, floating drydocks, fuel barges, and God knows what, were being assembled into an armada. Finally, ship after ship, the *Langfit* among them, then barges in tow, drydocks in tow, all assembled to form a huge flotilla like a floating city, made their way into the open sea to meet other ships to complete a convoy that stretched from horizon to horizon. With destroyers darting in and out and around the convoy to protect it from submarines, the armada began its creep to Tacloban on the island of Leyte in the Philippines. If this sight, so overwhelming, was but a side show to our main effort in Europe, I can't conceive of what the armada heading across the English Channel for the landings in Normandy must have been like. Even Yamamoto, who said that bombing Pearl Harbor would awaken a sleeping giant, could not have imagined how large the giant.

Tacloban — another harbor, another wait; ships being unloaded, ships being loaded, convoys being dismantled, convoys being formed. Leyte had fallen, Tacloban was becoming the new Hollandia. Ahead was the island of Luzon. Landings had been made there, but the island was yet to be secured. Fighting was chewing up supplies and men. Stuff and men had to get up there quickly. Slow convoys couldn't do it. Ships moving alone could.

I shipped out of Tacloban on a rusty hulk, a tramp steamer that had slipped out of Borneo just ahead of the Japanese. She had been plying the waters of the South Seas ever since, picking up cargo wherever its owner could make a buck. She was in the Philippine Sea making lone runs between Leyte and Luzon, carrying war supplies and men. With her motley crew of Malays, Negroes, Mulattoes, Chinese, Norwegians, and Aussies, she was a reincarnation of Joseph Conrad's *Narcissus*.

> But in truth they had been men who knew toil, privation, violence, debauchery — but knew not fear, and had no desire of spite in their hearts. Men hard to manage, but easy to inspire;

voiceless men — but men enough to scorn in their hearts the sentimental voices that bewailed the hardness of their fate. It was a fate unique and their own; the capacity to bear it appeared to them the privilege of the chosen! Their generation lived inarticulate and indispensable, without knowing the sweetness of affections or the refuge of a home — and died free from the the dark menace of a narrow grave. They were the everlasting children of the mysterious sea.

A description of the crew of
the *Narcissus,* by Joseph Conrad

We knew the dangers that these men faced carrying war cargoes; they knew the dangers we were to face. From worlds apart we fit together far more compatibly than we did with the Navy crews on the *Langfit,* who seemed to make a point of separating themselves from us. That may have been necessary. They had no time to get chummy. Still, the captain might have organized some entertainment, a skit or something, possibly some music. In all his crew there must have been some talent. We had been looking forward to the day we would cross the equator, hoping for some fun — a King Neptune ceremony complete with pranks, perhaps like getting our heads shaved — anything to acknowledge we were more than just cargo. When the day came, it was like any other, except for an announcement when the equator had been crossed.

On the tramp steamer, our *"Narcissus,"* the crew gathered on deck at night to sing sea chanteys. Picture it: roguish characters singing songs of the sea; the stars in the heavens; the black water around reflecting the stars; and beneath the surface Japanese submarines hunting for just such a ship to blow to bits. Who could escape the feeling that there was a God in heaven who held our souls in the palm of his hand? Pine away, Walter Mitty; here was adventure, here was romance; and I was there.

While I was caught up in my reverie, 20 weary men of the depleted 3rd Platoon of Company K of the 6th Division's 63rd Infantry were being shelled defending Hell's Hill on the island of Luzon. The whine of a shell coming in sent a soldier diving for cover in a hole already occupied by the platoon leader, landing on him and rupturing his kidney. For him, the war was over. For me, it meant the beginning.

I arrived at Company K fresh, clean, and green from the United States. The 3rd Platoon of Company K, veterans of battles in New Guinea and now the Philippines, were to meet their new platoon leader on Hell's Hill, an outpost blocking enemy attempts to get through to our rear.

From the soldier who guided me through brush and grasses and on up Hell's Hill to meet my platoon, I learned that the officers of the 63rd were respected, and in the case of Battalion Commander Major Arndt Mueller, both respected and feared. In New Guinea, according to my guide, Mueller, then Captain of Company K, was ordered to take forward his unit, not yet baptized by fire, to replace a badly battered company at the front. As they moved ahead, going to the rear were trucks piled high with the bodies of dead Americans, a sight that drained whatever courage these green soldiers had built up to sustain them in battle. Moving his company into position as night fell, Mueller made himself highly visible going from platoon to platoon and squad to squad and man to man, giving encouragement and checking emplacements. Then he entered the jungle ahead of the American lines to scout out Jap positions. Not a man in Company K had the guts to do what Mueller did, and they knew it. Next, having inspired confidence with this show of bravery, Mueller didn't wait to be attacked, he attacked. With information from his night of scouting, he outwitted the Japs. Blood flowed, Japanese blood. And so it was that I learned the legend of Major Mueller.

I have since been in touch with Mueller, now a retired Army Colonel living in Florida, who gave me the following and different version of what actually happened.

> It is interesting how the "legend" (as you put it) was created. I never considered myself a legend, but I know I had a reputation. At one of the reunions, one of our K Co. heroes greeted me with, "You were known as the meanest company commander and the whole division knew it!"
>
> "How come?"
>
> "We told them!"

The "legend" that your guide related probably came from a couple of incidents. I note that I was "both respected and feared." That part is no legend, especially the feared part. I think I know how that came about.

I joined the 63rd fresh out of South Dakota State. At State, despite my smallish size, I was co-captain of our conference champion football team. I was also named on the first string of the All-Conference team.

I came to the 63rd in pretty good physical shape, honed by seven years of football and baseball, no smoking, and only an occasional beer. I found the gruelling grind of football practice much tougher than any Army training I saw and the football discipline (at least on our team) was more severe than Army discipline I saw. Above all, football impressed me with the value and necessity of teamwork.

I was tough physically, self-confident, and maybe even cocky. I felt the burden of preparing Infantry troops for battle very intensely. I coined a phrase, "One drop of blood is more precious than ten gallons of sweat."

I set about making K Company training as tough as possible. I constantly dreamed up extra training, especially at night. And, of course, the troops knew the prescribed training schedule and they well knew when I piled on extra training. Believe me, that was not popular with the troops; they hated it, although my sergeants grudgingly admitted that the tougher training was better.

That was how the "feared" characterization was born. And we might as well add that I was hated during training. Of course, the troops loved to brag how rough things were in K Company — that certainly was part of the "legend."

Now as to the other part of your guide's account. Our first mission when deployed to the Lone Tree Hill area in New Guinea was to secure and defend a MASH unit supporting the division. Around dusk, after our perimeter was established, I took a walk outside our perimeter for two reasons. One, I wanted to see if there was any sign of Japs having sneaked up on us while we were busy, and two, to see how our perimeter defenses looked from the enemy viewpoint (always advisable to do). I found no sign of Japs and I did have to make some adjustments in our position to cover some vulnerabilities I had seen.

We had supplied our troops generously with hand grenades, because the doctrine for jungle defense at the time was to use hand grenades in the dark rather than small-arms fire. I don't remember how many grenades per man were issued, but about five would be a good guess. During the first night all hell broke loose — no small-arms fire but grenades popping all night long. There were reports of Japs here and Japs there.

At dawn I walked out in front of our positions, first making sure that my nervous troops knew I was there. I was looking for dead Japs, blood, bandages, trails — anything to indicate whether the Japs paid us a visit. I found nothing — absolutely nothing. I must confess I was really put out.

I immediately called a meeting of platoon leaders and platoon sergeants to demand that they go in front of our positions and bring me back some bodies or anything that would indicate that the Japs had been there. Of course they came back sheepishly empty-handed. I'm afraid that I ridiculed them and came down on them very hard.

I spent some time visiting with every soldier on the front line to hear each one's tale of what happened. What had happened was that some wallabies (small kangaroo-type animals) had thrashed around the jungle — maybe even having sexual encounters for all I know. My soldiers had used up almost all of the grenades issued — and didn't even get one wallaby! So for the next night I issued out a limited amount and kept the rest at the company [Command Post].

Units of the 1st and 20th Regiments were attacking Lone Tree Hill. (Why it was named that way, no one knows because it was a coral ridge covered with jungle. Someone said that one tree stood out above the rest.) The casualties from the 1st and 20th began to pour into MASH. What a bloody mess that was! My troops walked past the MASH like zombies with their eyes bugging and their mouths agape. So, I bid them to forego that sightseeing.

As if that was not enough, 2½-ton trucks began to roll in with bodies stacked like cordwood. The graves registration people, wearing gas masks, laid out the bodies immediately behind our lines so that they could identify and process them!

I told Rudy Brunsvold, our battalion commander, "After seeing that blood and gore at the MASH and then all those corpses, I don't know whether or not my troops will ever attack. Please get us the hell out of here as soon as you can!"

Soon my wish came to fruition; we were sent up to Lone Tree Hill to relieve two battalions of the 1st and 20th. Our battalion had more men than the two battalions put together. The place was a mess with Jap bodies littering the area. We tried to burn some of them, but that didn't work too well. We tried throwing some over a precipice, but got shot at — so that didn't work either. There were so many dead Japs that my bunkmate at night was a dead officer sprawled backwards over a fallen tree, whose body was alive with wriggling maggots.

When it came time to continue the offensive, K Company was elected to lead the attack of the battalion. Now comes the other event that probably led to your guide's "legend."

I attacked in the traditional — two [platoons] up and one back. My troops immediately went to the ground when the Japs opened fire. While ordering artillery fire (which didn't help much in the jungle), several bullets hit the tree above my head, according to my commo sgt. (who turned out to be the best PR man because he told all how calm I was, when I was scared to death). And I really didn't know what the hell to do.

So I did the traditional — I ordered the reserve platoon to envelope the Jap right flank (our left). The platoon couldn't outflank the Japs; they were only able to extend our line to the left, and then they too went to the ground.

So, all my splendidly trained troops were hugging the ground and hardly firing a shot. So, in desperation, I ran along the skirmish line of the entire company yelling at my troops to fire — shoot at the bushes and bottoms of trees. By the time I got to the left end of the line our fire sounded good, but no one was advancing. So I ran back down the line yelling, "Move — shoot, move!" Every four or five men, I kicked some prone soldier in the butt to get him moving. Shortly after I got to the right of the line, the movement stopped.

So, again I ran along the line to get the company moving. When I got to about the center of the line I suddenly found myself alone. Either there was a gap in our line or else I had become disoriented and was in front of the line. Suddenly, a hail of fire zipped at me. Fortunately, there was a huge fallen tree nearby. I ducked under its large trunk. Immediately, one machine-gun laced bullets along the left side of the trunk, followed by another which strafed the right side of the trunk.

Trapped under the tree by two machine-guns! I was sweaty, scared, and just plain miserable. What a neat trick, I thought. First, riflemen open up on a skirmish line; and then, when the troops take cover behind that convenient tree, the two machine-guns enfilade the line. How clever! Wonder if the Jap riflemen are advancing towards me under cover of the machine-gun fire? Boy, they can really knock me off!

I had an M1 rifle, but it was hard to use in my cramped position underneath the tree; nevertheless, I violated one of my cardinal rules to never fire a weapon without aiming at something — I triggered off a clip of ammunition in the general direction of the enemy without aiming. It only served to irritate the Japs into increasing their machine-gun fire.

The sun was receding in the west. Behind me I heard our battalion commander, Rudy Brunsvold, asking my whereabouts. The soldiers behind me replied that I had been up and down the line, but they didn't know where I was.

I yelled, "I'm here trapped under this log."

When Rudy came within sight I cautioned, "Stop, two machine-guns have me covered. If you get closer they'll get you."

He stopped, "I just want to tell you to hold up where you are. L Company will pass through in the morning."

"Roger, but you had better hurry back to your CP before dark or some of my nervous soldiers will shoot you."

With that he departed. I had work to do. How to get out of this predicament? All gunners fire in bursts. So I decided to attract their attention by waving my arms, hoping to induce them to fire some burst, and then roll out from under the tree. It worked. Immediately following their bursts I rolled madly out from under the tree for about 15-20 yards and then desperately raced for our lines with Jap fire trying to reach me [while] yelling for my soldiers not to fire.

My orders for the night were simple, "Dig in where you are. Left platoon curl back your open flank to protect yourselves from envelopment." (The right flank of the company was no worry because it rested on the edge of a precipice.)

I was thoroughly disappointed with the day's events. This highly trained company had advanced a hundred, at the most two hundred, yards all day against light fire.

I called a platoon leaders' meeting, which we held in the dark. "This has been a bad day, gentlemen. We will never win this war this way. We cannot let our men go to ground. When they do, they are out of sight, out of control, and they can't even shoot effectively. Our next time will come soon enough. When it does, we will use marching fire. For heaven's sake, there are enough trees so we can take cover behind them without going to ground. We can shoot from behind trees standing up or kneeling — but no prone position. It's up to us leaders to be in front with them leading them."

"It's that MASH back there," one of the platoon leaders exclaimed. "My men are scared to death. They're like zombies!"

As I anticipated, the battalion did not clear the ridge, so our turn came again quite soon. This time I attacked with platoons in column. I joined the lead platoon. Our marching fire was working quite well. Some of the riflemen fired at suspected ground targets, while some were detailed to watch for snipers in trees. The Jap snipers tied themselves in trees and usually fought until either killed or bypassed.

I had one startling experience. The area was loaded with what some called banyan trees. They had large "shoulders" [and] the Japs were taking cover behind [them]. As I stepped around one shoulder, which had many bullet holes in it, I was startled by a Jap in the prone position to my right. I swung my rifle around to shoot him, but something stopped me. The Jap wasn't moving. Upon closer examination I found that a bullet penetrated the shoulder and drilled through his head. Praise be for armor-piercing ammunition!

We cleared the ridge and dived off into a road leading to Sarmi airfield, which was our next objective. We advanced to the airfield without incident only to view an amazing sight. The "airfield" was a long strip of stumps from knee to waist high! This had not shown up in air photos. Everyone assumed this was an operational airfield or close to being one.

So I called Rudy Brunsvold, our battalion commander, "We're in control of the near end of the airfield."

"Proceed to clear and secure the entire airfield."

"I don't think that will be necessary. This is a field of knee-high and waist-high stumps."

Rudy was incredulous, but accepted my report and ordered me to hold up in place.

We had been up on Lone Tree Hill (ridge) in the mud and dirt several days. Our fatigues were dun-colored instead of green. The ditch by the road was filled with tan-colored water. I craved a bath; I felt filthy and funky. So I posted security, ripped off my clothes, invited my company in, [and] took a muddy bath and washed my fatigues. I felt great!

And K Company had begun to operate like it should.

I think the "legend" was born of the events I have related to you.

The "legend" as I heard it may not have been accurate, but it told me what to expect. What Major Mueller demanded of himself he would demand of his officers. I felt sick. I didn't come to be brave, to be a hero; I came for an adventure, and now it dawned on me — Mueller would want heroes, and I wasn't sure I was up to it. The injured lieutenant I was to replace turned out to be none other than Norwood G. (for God), described to me as a blond, blue-eyed guy, the epitome of the kind of soldier, both in mind and body, that Adolf Hitler wanted in his army. In fact, he admired German soldiers. The Germans in turn would have admired him. That he won a battlefield commission says all that needs to be said about his soldiering. What a spot to be in. Not only did I have to meet the standards set by a battalion commander who was a legend, I had to fill the shoes of a guy commissioned in battle. Before the night was over, the Japs were to give me an opportunity to show my colors.

Chapter 9

Baptism

AFTER A HALF HOUR or so of hiking and listening to my guide's stories, we began making our way along a path cut through bamboo grass bordering a stream about ten yards to our right. We were coming up on a place where the stream narrowed. On the other side, the Japanese were encamped in Montalban, a barrio of grass huts mounted high on poles, ideal platforms for snipers to pick us off. So much for hearing about legends. Silence was now important. We hunched down low in the grass to keep from being seen. Once past Montalban we soon reached the base of the hill and started to climb, leaving the protection of the grass for less-protective scraggly trees and shrubs. As we got within a hundred or so yards of the outpost, trip wires attached to land mines placed by our troops as a line of defense had to be detached and reattached for us to get through. My guide, in a voice showing about as much concern as someone trying to remember where their car keys were, mumbled, "Now let's see, I think there's one here where the path turns left," and "Whoops, there was one back there we didn't see. Glad we didn't trip it." So was I.

We passed a Japanese body with maggots crawling out its eyes, ears, and gut where it had been ripped open. We rounded a curve — two more bodies, up ahead more dead Japs, all bloated and stinking. I thought of a dead dog I had seen floating down the Niagara River when I was a kid. I felt no more for them than I did for the dog. At the top we arrived at an area of about half an acre, a moonscape, minus vegetation, except for shattered tree stumps and a few denuded bushes. It was a desert, complete with gopher holes — man-sized gopher holes. As we passed a hole, a muddy helmet would rise just enough for the face under it to stare at me momentarily, then retreat to the shelter of mother earth. At the so-called Command Post, which was just a bigger hole, a handsome soft-spoken lad beckoned me to jump in quickly, warning me that the Japanese were constantly on the alert to shoot at anything that moved. Sergeant Johnson introduced himself as the platoon sergeant. He might have been 20 — he looked a boyish 18, just a kid — yet here he was burdened by more responsibility than most adults will ever assume in a lifetime, responsibility where the life and death of men depended on his decisions and leadership.

I had been fighting the urging of my bowels, but thinking less about my problem and more of me as a target that would attract enemy fire, Johnson urged me to wait. "It's getting dark. Night comes on fast. In a few minutes it will be dark. You'll be less likely to be seen." Whether from fear or nature's natural call, I couldn't wait. The wonder was that I hadn't filled my pants already. I was wearing coveralls given me at the Infantry School at Fort Benning, Georgia. Compare, if you will, the advantages of just dropping your pants while squatting versus having to drop your entire coveralls and get them stuffed between your legs and out of the way. My lily-white body appeared on the top of the hill in the dusk like a full moon rising. A perfect target. All hell broke loose. Mortar shells started dropping around me. A machine-gun opened up. Within ten seconds I had dropped my coveralls, completed my mission, and pulled them back up — no doubt a record.

This map, from Colonel Mueller's collection, indicates the proposed plan for attacking and capturing Hill 400, or Hell's Hill. Plan One called for a route through forests; Plan Two called for a direct approach. The second plan was chosen.

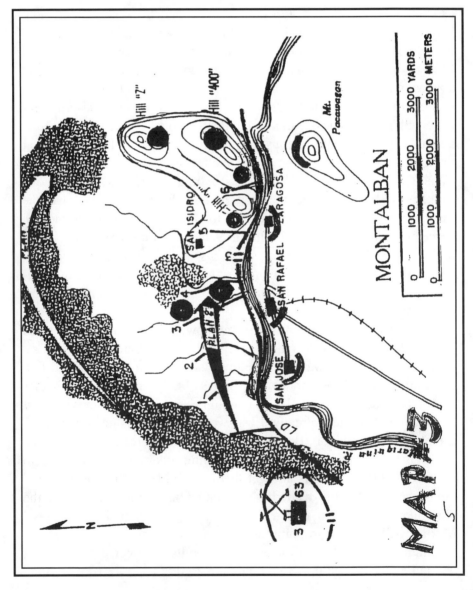

The firing was the opening shots of an all-out Japanese effort to take the outpost. Round after round of artillery exploded around us. In the din I could hardly hear Johnson, who was trying to tell me he was anxious for me to take command. Here I had been worried that he might resent my taking over, possibly preempting his chance for a field commission. He wanted no part of either. With no opportunity to look around, I had no idea where our men were positioned or how our defenses were organized. I told Johnson I would take the responsibility for what happened, but he would have to tell me what he thought we should do.

The shelling intensified; then it stopped. Japs came screaming. We were 25 or so; they seemed like 2,025. But 2,000 or 200, our machineguns were beautifully placed. We mowed them down in our crossfire, though some were probably getting through. Who knew? Now dark, with the dust kicked up from the shelling obscuring what little moonlight there was, I couldn't see anything from our hole. Should I, the new officer in charge, get out and try to assess the situation? I wouldn't have been able to see anything. And I wouldn't have known what to look for. Anything moving above ground would appear to be Japs. If the Japs didn't get me, our men would. I stayed put and relied on Sergeant Johnson. He had his rifle ready to shoot, should anything come our way. Otherwise, he seemed to be taking it all in stride.

Major Mueller called on the radio, probably wondering whether his new lieutenant had cracked. I radioed back that I had once been mobbed by a bunch of women in a department store Christmas sale, and that was worse than this. What baloney. How stupid. I should have told him the truth, that I was scared out of my wits, that I had learned I was totally unsuited for this kind of work. I was to pay for being a wiseguy. My bravado suggested to Mueller that I was just the person to lead a wild adventure he was cooking up in his head.

I didn't need to be there on Hell's Hill. Forty-eight hours before, while on my way to the 63rd, I was pulled aside by an adjutant at division headquarters, who had noted my medical background on my service record. He told me there was a desperate shortage of Medical Officers and asked me if I would be willing to take over a Battalion Aid Station. Working in an operating room as an enlisted man, I had become good at tying off bleeders. Hitting a vein with a needle was one of my

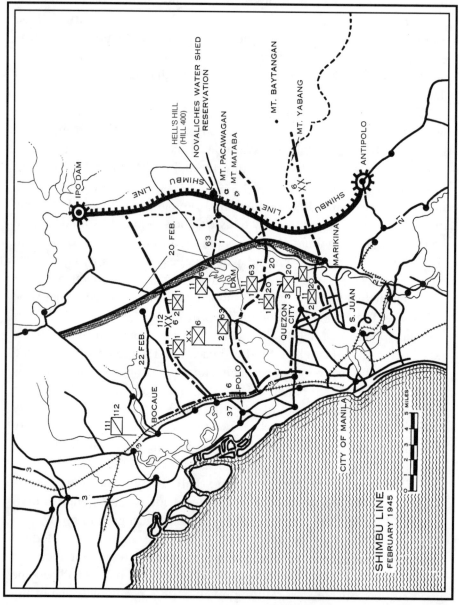

From 6th Infantry Division Public Relations Section, *The 6th Infantry Division in World War II, 1939-1945.* (Washington, D.C.: Infantry Journal Press, 1947)

SHIMBU LINE
FEBRUARY 1945

Hill X at the Shimbu Line. (From *The 6th Infantry Division in World War II*)

specialties; administering plasma would have been no problem. But the whole idea struck me as ridiculous. I misunderstood. I was not being asked to be a surrogate surgeon. I was being asked to be the Administrative Officer of an aid station. Only years later did I learn that the table of organization for an aid station included an Administrative Officer. Had I understood the duties, I might have taken the job. When I turned the medical job down, the adjutant asked me what made me think I would be a good combat officer. I told him I was worried that I might not be, but I wanted to try. I got the job. (Later in life as a career counselor, I often cited this conversation as proof that candor in an interview can help get a job.) I had passed the point of no return and was in the thick of it.

Around us, above us, who knew where, we seemed to be overrun. Our situation was exactly like one I had seen in an Army training film. The defenders were in foxholes somewhat protected from artillery fire, while the attackers were above ground vulnerable to shell fire. The defenders' commander, if I remembered the film correctly, called for his artillery to fire on his position, reasoning that his men were protected while the attackers were not. I called for our artillery to fire on ours. Whether they did or did not fire on us I don't know, but shells seemed to be landing closer with more intensity.

At midnight? 3:00 a.m.? I only remember the night as an eternity. As suddenly as the battle began, it stopped. Had the Japanese just backed off into the darkness? We didn't know. Whether they had retreated 10 feet or 1,000 feet, we didn't know. They may have given up to attack another night. We didn't know. They may have been regrouping for another assault. We didn't know.

They had tried to destroy our defenses on our right, and they had been successful. Men key to our defense there were dead men. That the Japanese had successfully breached our defenses, they didn't know. They departed, possibly maneuvering to try to break through on our left. We didn't know.

They could be silent, like a cat stalking its prey, or act wild and crazy like hyenas, tearing apart their victims. It was silent, but was it the silence of a battle spent or the silence of cats creeping in the dark ready to spring on their victims? We didn't know.

Not knowing made the silence terrible. Johnson and I began to talk.

He told me about himself. He was a farm lad from down along the Ohio River. Although we couldn't see each other in the dark, from the tone of his voice I could almost see the smile on his face as he reminisced about his life there, especially when he told about going to high school just a couple of years back. We got around to discussing our military situation.

The men were spent. Our ammunition was spent. It had to be replenished. The company commander called us on the radio; help was on the way. If it was to reach us, a way had to be cleared through the mine fields. Staff Sergeant Lanham had set the mines. The lot to remove them fell to him. But why couldn't we wait just a few more hours to daylight? Why couldn't we gamble on the Japs not coming back? The chance of deactivating the mines at night was poor at best. The chance of setting one off and getting killed was good. And if the Japs *were* still around, anyone who ventured beyond our perimeter would surely be spotted. What was to be gained? These thoughts must have been going through Lanham's mind. We can't know, but it is easy to imagine that he might have felt he was being asked to give up his life for something that struck him as stupid.

Lanham had already been through the worst of the battle, or battles. This was not his first night of hell on Hell's Hill. To push him to clear the mines was to push him to the point where, if he didn't blow a mine, he might blow a mental fuse. Like the Civil War youth in Stephen Crane's *The Red Badge of Courage*, who had been paralyzed with fright and ran from the enemy's charge, Lanham could have frozen in his tracks. Or like the same youth at another time, who against all odds led a wild charge against the enemy, he could have irrationally and impulsively charged the mine field, tripping one mine after another. That would have been the easy way to become a hero. The hard way was to suppress terrible fear, say a prayer, and do the job. Lanham cleared the mines.

I can see him even now out there in no-man's-land, flashlight in hand, crawling around searching for mines. He despaired. "I can't find the goddamn things." Somebody yelled an Army kind of encouragement: "Lanham, you sonofabitch, you put the goddamn mines out there." Another yelled, "Lanham, you sonofabitch, don't give up." So it went. Lanham cursed, and the men cursed their encouragement. Not a man

Major Mueller sent out constant patrols before and after the capture of Hill 400, one of which I led. There was a need to document enemy activities, troop locations, and resources, a need to gather information should the battalion participate in an attack on Ipo Dam, and a need for constant American activity to keep the enemy off base and confused about American strength, especially after mid-March when units on the flanks had been transferred elsewhere, leaving the Third Battalion vulnerable.

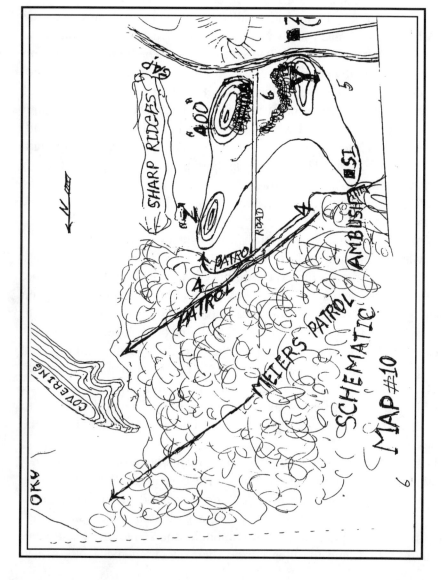

among us had the guts to be out there doing the job Lanham was doing, and each of us knew it.

Dick Fleming, Captain of Company K, said Lanham should get a medal for his night's work, and told me to write up what had happened. In *The 6th Infantry Division in World War II*, published by the Infantry Journal Press, the writers used many of these citations to describe battle scenes. Among them is my description of Sergeant Lanham:

> Staff Sergeant Charles H. Lanham was a squad leader of a platoon that was cut off from all friendly forces by a strong counterattacking enemy force, the only possible approach to the platoon's hilltop position being a steep brush-covered trail that had been extensively mined during the day. While a platoon of reinforcements awaited the signal to advance to the beleaguered troops, Lanham made his way down the trail groping for trip wires in total darkness. Knowing that his platoon needed immediate aid, he hurried the job by standing and using a flashlight that revealed his position to numerous enemy snipers. Lanham deactivated seven mines and detonated two but was unable to locate the last one. Rather than delay the reinforcement any longer, he boldly walked down the path in the area where he knew the unexploded mine must be, and hit the trip wire with his foot, exploding a phosphorous grenade but miraculously escaping injury. He then quickly led the supporting platoon up the hill to aid in repulsing the enemy attack. Lanham was awarded the Distinguished Service Cross, second only to the Congressional Medal of Honor for bravery.

Lanham survived, but I never saw him again. I can guess what happened. In a war of thousands of mini-dramas, an incident involving one of Major Mueller's lieutenants has to be one of the most poignant incidents of mental suffering. It told a lot about Mueller's leadership, and gave me the clue to Lanham's fate. The 6th Division, which fought the bloodiest battle of the New Guinea campaign, was, nevertheless, seldom engaged in big and famous battles, fighting most of the time in a grinding war ferreting out the enemy's hidden enclaves, driving them out of

Japanese caves at the Shimbu Line. (From *The 6th Infantry Division in World War II*)

caves with explosives and flames, constantly patrolling, flushing them out of their hideaways in the thick brush, and pursuing them up narrow mountain roads where they had every landmark along the line of their retreat targeted for our arrival. The 6th's job was to knock the enemy off in small engagements, one after another. The Division fought 219 days of continuous combat on Luzon, averaging 100 enemy casualties per day, to establish the record for the Pacific. Day after day of warfare, whether a day of a skirmish or a major engagement, whether a day of no action or only the threat of action, ground down the men of the 6th. Men came to the end of their endurance.

Mueller, always on the alert for this to happen to men in his battalion, and suspecting something amiss in one of his units that wasn't getting its jobs done, went to investigate. Approaching, and seeing the officer in charge praying his rosary, he held back, not wanting to disturb a man in prayer. The anguish of the officer was obvious. He had been a fine officer, leading the troops through New Guinea and all of the Luzon campaign, but now was at the end of his rope. I was not in New Guinea — I

Major Mueller on the left planning a strategy at the Shimbu Line. (From *The 6th Infantry Division in World War II*)

came in during the middle of the Luzon, Philippines, campaign — yet it is easy for me to put myself in his shoes.

His finger was on the first bead, as he began praying, "Hail Mary, full of Grace, the Lord is with thee. Blessed art thou among women. . . ." His lips kept moving automatically saying the words. His mind drifted off. "God help me. God rid me of this fear. Don't let me be a coward." Trembling fingers moved forward from bead to bead. "Holy Mary, Mother of God, have mercy on me." His lips kept moving while his mind drifted to his men. He knew he was spent, too confused to make a good decision. Were the men already killed because of some mistake he had made? "God help me, I can't send any more men to their death. God don't let me die." Here was a man who had been a good officer. Some would say, "Court-martial him if he doesn't shape up. What he needs is a good kick in the rear." But he is spent and no one can change that. And up to that time he had been a fine officer.

Major Mueller saw those trembling fingers moving from bead to bead, he saw his face, the blank stare, the tears in his eyes. This was a time for reward, not punishment, for a man who had given his all. Mueller found him another assignment where the officer would continue contributing to the war effort with effiency and with honor.

While Lanham was working his way down from our position, Sergeant Thomas Alva Edison Atchley and his platoon were working their way up to reenforce us. Tom also used a flashlight to pick their way through mined areas. They made better targets than my lily-white body, but they got through OK. Atchley was awarded a Silver Star for his part in the action, and shortly after was awarded a battlefield commission.

Tom Atchley was from a small town in Arkansas. When the war was over he returned home, never to leave it again, much to the disappointment of the men of his platoon who tried to get him to come to unit reunions. He was short, good-looking, and always smiling; everyone liked him. He was one of these people who, when you are talking to them, give you feeling they are intensely interested in what you have to say. He himself was laconic, only talking when he had something positive to offer and to make you feel things were going to be OK. Every man reaches a point where he is at the end of his endurance, where he can't take any more, but Atchley was a rock. He had been in all the campaigns from the beginning to the end, yet he never faltered, was always steady. He may have been a religious man, I don't know. I never heard him swear. If he was ever afraid — and he must have been at times — he faced it with an inner strength that came through to the men and gave them strength. Battle marks men like Tom as leaders. They are the glue that bonds men together into a fighting unit. Among the rank and file, ordinary men from ordinary places, the Atchleys and the Johnsons emerged in combat as leaders around whom men would rally to form a team capable of performing extraordinary acts.

In 1995, as I write this, there is a move to include women in combat units. I am a man who has lost two wives after long periods of fighting cancer, and it seems to me that they suffered through it all with a fortitude that I am not sure we men possess. They demonstrated the best qualities of a soldier. Yet from seeing men like Atchley, it strikes me that the success of an Infantry unit relies on an all-male chemistry, requiring a leader who is a catalyst for bringing out the best in men to form a bond so strong they will give up their lives for another. Call it male chauvinism, and it probably is, but I believe women in an Infantry company might spoil the chemistry.

When dawn came to Hell's Hill, the Japs did not return. The crossfire from our machine-guns had mowed them down by the hundreds before they had penetrated our perimeter, leaving Jap bodies strewn about like trees smashed in an avalanche. Wandering around at the break of dawn to assess our situation, I came face to face with an Oriental. I raised my rifle to kill him, but was stopped by one of our soldiers. In our company as elsewhere, Filipinos, some just youngsters in their teens, would attach themselves to us and fight alongside. As I went about I expected only Johnson and myself to be alive from our platoon, but only three men — those defending the right side of our perimeter — were dead. More were wounded, one moaning pitifully, begging his buddy to finish him off. Mercifully, death came shortly on its own.

Holding the hill was proving costly. What we didn't know was that we were overlooking the headquarters of General Kobayashi, commander of the Shimbu Line, a major Japanese defense position on Luzon. Some of our men had noticed signs of activity, so a .50-caliber machine-gun was dragged into position to fire whenever anyone was seen. The Japanese were too far out of range for us to do much harm, but the general didn't like being shot at, which helps explain why he expended so many men trying to kick us off. Later, captured documents revealed that we faced the remnants of a 1,000-odd-man Japanese regiment and a medium (150mm) mortar battalion of 12 mortars. We were about 20 men, about half strength — always at half strength.

I thought the hill was being abandoned because we were ordered to leave. It seemed to me that getting the wounded off the hill and making our way out carrying ammunition and supplies was going to be so difficult that I couldn't see how we were going to manage the dead. I said something to Johnson about leaving them behind, a thought that should have been kept to myself, judging from the look on his face. Quickly, I switched the subject to how we would get these men back, not whether we should. Soldiers' bodies were sacred. If we didn't bring them back, my chance of gaining the respect of these men was nil. My feeling for my own body was, and still is, that from dust I am and to dust I shall return. Where I drop is good enough for me. But obviously, this wasn't the place to expound my philosophy.

Soldiers will do almost anything to bring back a body from battle. It's a duty they owe to a comrade. But they're not morbid. A soldier would lose a best friend and within an hour link up with another soldier and be chatting away as if nothing had happened. It had to be like that to keep going.

As it turned out, we were only being relieved. Troops on the hill were rotated every few days. Commenting on the situation years later Mueller said, "I still get the shivers up my back when I think how the soldiers of the 3rd Battalion fought in that area all by themselves after the Division decided the area was too tough and shifted the offense to the area we [finally] went to next — where hills A, B, and X were located" — hills that I would learn plenty about later.

At any rate, my first battle was over. I had met the enemy who had ravaged Asia, who had raped Manchuria, and I now I felt I had been raped. I was no longer the virgin lieutenant. And for better or for worse, the 3rd Platoon of Company K of the 3rd Battalion of the 63rd Infantry of the 6th Division had a new leader. I was an officer, the lowest of the low, the last link in a long chain of command, the link that connects to the men who do the fighting that determines the outcome of battles. If the platoon leaders aren't any good, the entire chain isn't worth a damn. My role that first night wasn't enough for the men to size me up, but at least I hadn't blundered, thanks to the look on Johnson's face that kept me from doing something stupid. A time did come when the platoon decided to kill me, but that story will have to wait.

Chapter 10

Birthday Party

N THE LETTER that Mueller had sent to me to dispel, or at least correct, "the legend" that had developed relating to him, he wrote that he was hated during training. But in the Army the word hate isn't necessarily synonymous with loathing. To say, "God, I hate that Mueller," in translation means, "You think you got it tough. Nobody drives men harder than Mueller. We're the toughest outfit in the Army." What I got from the men was a sense of pride in serving under a tough soldier. "He is always up front, in the lead." And in years to come, that pride turned to affection. He became a magnet drawing veterans of the 3rd Battalion to reunions, especially men from Company K, his command before his promotion. Men made their way to see him in Florida where he retired. I made the pilgrimage. From this trip and from an extensive correspondence I learned what made him tick as a commander, and it was probably just as well I didn't know what went on in his brain during the war, or I would have been even more scared of what lay ahead.

During the war I saw only Major Mueller the soldier — always checking on us, our weapons, our position. He never stopped being a soldier. Never once did I see him without his helmet, and I would have hated for him to see me not wearing mine. When things were quiet in our sector he often seemed to disappear. The troops said he was probably off where there was some action, that if there was a battle somewhere he had to go and see it, see if he could learn something about the way the Japs fought. They were probably right. I always thought of him as the consummate soldier, a man never out of motion, never out of fatigues, never without a helmet. You can't imagine what it was like when I met him years later in Florida, a smiling, well-dressed gentleman in a good-looking yellow sport coat with points of a tan handkerchief sticking out of his breast pocket. And he was soft-spoken, not the matter-of-fact major whose direct way of giving orders told us he meant business. We met for lunch at the La Playa resort near Naples, Florida, our conversation ranging, as you might suspect, from, "Did you ever hear from so and so after the war?" and "Do you remember the time we made that night attack on Hill A?" I had been curious about one thing and thought he might fill me in. I had been in the hospital, and when I returned to the company I learned that four or more men had been swept away trying to cross a stream. Mueller immediately responded that this had happened because he had made a bad decision. No pulling of punches, just "I made a bad decision."

The company had been making its way along a road in northern Luzon leading to the town of Kiangan, reputed to be the headquarters of General Yamashita. At one point the road narrowed to a gorge cut through by a raging stream. A bluff ahead gave the Japs an excellent perch for interdicting fire. So Mueller ordered Company K across the stream where there was a good spot for them to provide covering fire. His supply sergeant had produced a rope, and Sergeant Munson of the Weapons platoon, an excellent swimmer, had stripped and was able to make his way across the turbulent waters. Having found that he could touch bottom along the way, and having secured the rope across the stream, it seemed logical that men with gear and weapons could make it across holding on to the rope. The equipment the men carried made the difference. Their feet went out from under them and four were swept away.

I hadn't meant to, but I had brought back an unhappy memory. Obviously he dwelled on it because he followed up our visit with a long letter going through the whole story again. He need not have dwelled so on what he considered a bad decision. It sounded more like a good decision that had unexpectedly gone wrong. And he had made so many good decisions that had saved so many lives that I felt compelled to follow up with a letter that said,

> It must be, should be, very satisfying to you to have old-timers like me seek you out. It says, "This is an important man in our lives. Time and again he put his life on the line and time and again he had to send us out to put our lives on the line. Our lives were in his hands. With courage and wisdom he got us through." Some of course didn't make it. I don't care if you combined the genius of Clausewitz, Alexander the Great, and Robert E. Lee, in no way could you have fought the war without something going amiss.

I went on to say that the remarkable thing was that he was right so often and that the men knew it. They knew they were fortunate to have him as their leader.

Mueller was touched by my letter and wrote to tell me so. Then he picked up on what I said about the great generals:

> You mentioned Clausewitz, Lee, and Alexander the Great. Took me back in time to when I attended a little one room country school. It had a small library in the back of the room. Someone had placed in it a book of the great battles of history. So before I entered high school in town I had become familiar with Thermopylae, Hannibal at Canne, Alexander the Great at Arbella; and Austerlitz, Chancellorsville, Antietam, Gettysburg, and others — and the lessons each had for us. Thus, I became interested in strategy and tactics and the qual-

ities of leadership. This led me to further investigation of the art and science of war in high school, but with only limited access to such literature.

Our university library was much better. I became familiar with Genghis Khan, Attila the Hun, the Ostrogoths, the Visigoths, and the Vandals. I found that the WWI battles did not have much to offer except for Von Hindenburg and Ludendorf at the Battle of Tannenberg and the Masurian Lakes. So, by the time I came to the 63rd Infantry, I was well versed in the Principles of War: the Objective, Mass, Maneuver, Economy of Force, Offensive, Unity of Command, Simplicity, Security, and Surprise.

The Mueller "legend" had inspired us to follow him; the great men of military history had inspired him to be audacious, to do the unorthodox, to do the unexpected, and as a result he often concocted some of the damnedest missions to keep the enemy confused and off base. He would attack at night, something Americans seldom did. He sent out patrols to harass and confuse the enemy. This was the man I had yet to meet. He was off somewhere when I joined Company K. Then he sent for me to give me some kind of an orientation — so I thought.

When I arrived at Company K, no one told me what was going on, where we were located, where the Japs were, nothing of the immediate tactical situation. Dick Fleming, the Company's Captain, had told me I was to be the leader of the 3rd Platoon and that a guide would shortly take me up to them where they were dug in on the top of Hell's Hill. Writing to me years later, Mueller confessed that this was a hell of a thing to do and read the riot act to Fleming for sending me into a hornet's nest on my first day with the Company. It may not have been a bad thing. What's the expression about banging your head against the wall because then it feels so good to stop? The days immediately following the battle on Hell's Hill were relatively free from combat, but full of the discomforts of sleeping on the ground, baking in the hot sun, getting soaked with rain, being chewed by insects, and general misery — the kind that can grind soldiers down as much as combat. For me, these miseries, at least for a time, were a welcome relief.

All I knew at that time was that from Hell's Hill we could see

Japanese milling about upstream just close enough to annoy them with
.50-caliber machine-gun fire, but too far away to hit them with any accu-
racy. Farther on was a dam, one I was told incorrectly was Ipo. This
information, which like so much incorrect information I was to pick up,
led me to the wrong conclusion about our mission and what I could
expect. Platoon Sergeant Johnson had told me that Ipo was the source of
Manila's water supply, now cut off by the Japs, creating a desperate situation for that city. Hastily dug wells and jury-rigged pumps trying to
supply water were neither bountiful nor sanitary. Typhoid fever threatened. The dam was a fortress of solid concrete about 150 feet high and
twice as wide. Even if we could get to it, the Japs were sure to have had
it mined and would blow it up before letting it get captured intact.
Nevertheless, I had heard that capturing it was a primary objective, and
I presumed I had been called to some kind of a briefing about assaulting
the dam.

Our speculation was somewhat off the mark. What we didn't know
was that Hell's Hill, officially Hill 400, was one of three high hill land
masses — the others were Mts. Pacawagan and Mataba — that the
Division was trying to take in a major effort to crack the Shimbu Line.
This effort, if successful, would have solved the problems of the dam.
Only the 3rd Battalion, assigned to Hell's Hill, had succeeded in accom-
plishing its mission. Forces were being shifted around for another
approach, leaving the 3rd Battalion holding Hell's Hill, its northern
flank now exposed with the withdrawal of troops there — a situation that
made Major Mueller uncomfortable. He was not the kind to sit and wait
for something to happen. A series of patrols were organized to penetrate
Japanese territory for two reasons: one to determine what he knew about
the Japanese forces, and the other to keep them off base with continual
American activity within their territory.

None of this did I know at the time, and knowing it now makes me
realize how naive it was for me to think that Major Mueller would take
a platoon leader into his confidence and lay out major battle plans and
strategies, interesting as it might have been. Too interesting, perhaps. I
am not sure it would have been a good idea for the troops to know that
we were somewhat isolated from other supporting units against an
enemy whose intentions and strengths were unknown. Nevertheless, I
was told to report to Major Mueller.

This drawing from Colonel Mueller's files depicts possible approaches to the capture of Mts. Mataba and Pacawagan, keystones in the Japanese defense, and shows the location of Hills A, B, and X, terrain ideally suited for locating defensive positions. Eventually efforts were concentrated on Hill A. In a charge — or more accurately a crawl — led by me, Hill A fell, after which the remaining defenses tumbled relatively quickly.

Mueller spread an aerial photo between us, pointing to some dark spots on a ridge. Tracing his finger along a stream leading to the ridge, he gave me the good news. "I want you to lead a patrol up this stream to this ridge, then climb it. The Air Corps thinks these black spots are caves where ammunition and supplies are being stored for the defense of Ipo. They have been bombing the hell out of the area to destroy them. Check to see if they are caves, and if so, find out what's in them. Also evaluate the effectiveness of their bombing. When you get to the top, start down the other side and find out what is going on right here," he said, pointing to a spot on the aerial photo that looked like holes dug in an embankment. "I'll give you Lonesome Polecat as a scout. He's a Chippewa and damned good. It should take you a day to get there and a day to get back. Take a radioman along, but be careful about using it because you don't want to give yourself away." So much for my orientation. So much for learning the tactical situation.

Jesus, Mueller was sending me deep into Jap territory. It was my own damn fault for making smartass remarks during the banzai attack on Hell's Hill. Now he would find out if his new lieutenant still thought that getting caught up in the rush of women in a department store was worse than fighting the Japs. And I would find out that this would be just the first of other missions cooked up by a military genius who was constantly thinking of ways to outwit the enemy.

We awakened at dawn on March 30, 1945, ready to leave on our patrol. It's a date I won't forget. It was my 26th birthday. I awoke with a sore throat and a fever. I could have turned myself into the medics, but I wouldn't.

Had I wanted a mission right out of a Kenneth Roberts novel about the French and Indian Wars, I had one, for better or for worse, and I was stuck with it. We started up the stream, two scouts in front followed by me, flankers to the sides to check the thick bamboo along the banks, riflemen and the radioman following, 22 in all — everything according to the manual — and everything arranged for the Japs to identify the leader and pick him off, an unpleasant thought that spoiled any romantic notions about our adventure.

One mile, two miles, three — we were getting deeper into Japanese territory. Lonesome Polecat dropped his right arm down, his palm extended, the signal for us to freeze. On a bluff ahead he had spotted a lone figure. I couldn't see him. He pointed to the highest tree as a point of reference, then talked me across the landscape tree by tree until I saw. My God, what he saw was just a pin on the landscape. It was true what they said about Indian scouts' telescopic eyes. The men said Lonesome could smell Japs. Up north in the mountains later in the campaign, the company was making its way up a narrow road hemmed in by thick vegetation. Lonesome suddenly jumped into the brush and came out dragging out a Jap who was caught with his pants down, literally.

Whoever it was on the bluff ahead departed. Perhaps he saw us. Perhaps he didn't. I raised my right arm and swept it forward and downward, the signal to move out. We moved as a unit. Not a man hesitated. Good God, back in the States where I had just come from I'd get whining from men told to clean their barracks. These men must have known there was a good chance we would never get back, yet they followed without hesitation.

We got to the ridge and climbed. The black spots on Mueller's photo were caves, storage places for ammunition and supplies, as predicted. Amazingly, they were not guarded. Apparently the Japs didn't expect a bunch of Americans to come prowling around. They might expect the caves to be bombed, so why have troops around to get killed? As for the bombing, it was ineffective. All it did was tear up the landscape.

Now all we had to do was climb down the ridge on the other side and see what the other black spots on the aerial photo were all about. The bombing, however, had so smashed up rocks and trees in an area already difficult to navigate that we couldn't move ahead without stumbling and falling. We were making too much noise, and it was getting dark. We stopped halfway down the ridge. In the quiet we could hear Japs talking below. Or thought we did. At night the rustle of a leaf, the noise of an animal, is the enemy heard; a protruding rock or the branch of a tree is the enemy seen. It takes disciplined men not to panic, not to shoot and give themselves away. These were disciplined men.

About midnight my throat began to tickle. I tried to suppress a cough. I coughed. I coughed, again. I coughed and coughed and coughed. The more I tried not to, the more I coughed. Oh God, please help me. I fought back tears. I was scared for my own life, and there were these men. What to do? To try to stumble away to rid myself of them would have made more noise than staying. And who was to know? Japs cough, too. If they heard me they might think it one of their own. I tried to think of what else I might do, then I realized the reason I could think was because I had stopped coughing.

Dawn came with just enough light to see 10, maybe 12 Japs, 30 feet below. We came crashing, charging down the hill and attacked. They were starting fires to cook breakfast. Their weapons were stacked along the bank where they had dug crude shelters. They never had a chance.

Our work done, I gave every officer's favorite order, "Let's get the hell out of here." This we did on the double, pausing only now and then to take a swig of water from our canteens, already nearly drained. Knowing there was a stream ahead, one we were to follow to get back to company headquarters, we began dreaming of water. I was worried about sunstroke or heat prostration. We needed a drink badly, but I worried more about the water. Some, maybe all, were going to want a drink without waiting the 20 minutes it would take to purify the water with a halogen pill. From my medical days, words like schistosomiasis popped into my head. I had visions of half my platoon dying a horrible death in some hospital.

Would the men wait the 20 minutes for a pill to work? These were well-disciplined troops, but telling them not to drink from what appeared to be clear flowing water might strike them as ridiculous. And apart from my concern for their health, I didn't want to be put in a position of giving an order I couldn't enforce. When we got to water at last, the stream was strewn with dead and rotting water buffalo. The Japs had been killing animals and dragging them into streams to pollute our drinking water. Seeing these bloated carcasses floating about, each man filled his canteen, dropped in the pill, and waited the 20 minutes.

The next day, one of our privates, a sweet, gentle, and not very bright guy, felt compelled to get something off his chest. "Lieutenant, when you wouldn't stop coughing we decided to kill you. I hope you wouldn't have taken it personal."

Chapter 11

Respite

NOW I HAD TWO memorable experiences under my belt, but my first night with Company K, the night on Hell's Hill, was the worst of the war. At the time, I thought every day was going to be like it, one raging battle after another. That's the way it is in the movies. There is, however, the matter of logistics. Artillery supporting us during the battle for Hell's Hill used ammunition at such a rate that ordnance trucks had to work half the night bringing up ammunition from the rear to keep the guns firing. But even rear ammo dumps can keep a battle like this supplied for only so long. In the final analysis, supplies had to keep coming over a long line moving from depot to depot, starting with one in the United States. Lucky for us we had those supply lines.

And just as lucky for us, Japanese supply lines back to Japan were cut. But they had by no means shot their wad. The caves we saw were just a part of hundreds — thousands — of others tucked away in the mountains of Luzon. But, here, on the Shimbu Line (I had at last learned the name of our battle area), the Japanese supplies were depleted. All would be quiet for awhile; quiet enough for Major Mueller to think up something like a patrol or some way to annoy the Japs — he never wasted an opportunity keep them off base or to pick up some information that might be useful. During these quiet periods, Division headquarters often requested a platoon for some special duty, usually some easy assignment. Mueller received such a request. I had done my bit with the patrol; now it was my turn to get something easy.

Manila had been recaptured, but there were still stray Japanese in the city, particularly in the old walled part. They were too starved to cause any trouble, yet they made people nervous. Off we went, two jeeploads of us, rifles in hand, technically headed for combat — in fact, looking forward to a spree. All we found in the old city was rubble. If there were any Japs there, what was needed was a headstone to show where they were buried. In Manila itself, downtown was a mess, making it difficult at times to get by buildings that had been blown up, some lying in the streets closing them off. The once proud Great Eastern Hotel stood like a skeleton, its framework intact but nothing else — no windows, no floors, no roof. Yet in one of the worst sections of the city, rising from the ashes and all spruced up for the grand reopening, was The New Chicago Lunch. Man's resiliency inspires hope. Buffalo, my hometown, had a New Chicago Lunch. I used to see it as I passed by on a streetcar on my way home from work. It always looked forlorn, reminding me of the painting by Edward Hopper in which he portrayed two people seated by the window of a restaurant, the only sign of life in an otherwise dark and deserted urban setting. The New Chicago Lunch in Buffalo was a depressing sight; here in Manila, seeing it lifted one's spirits.

Wandering around Manila, we came across the Stork Club, the 21, Club Manila, and other similarly sleazy places with equally pretentious names. The Joy Happiness Club sounded classy, so we checked it out. No one seemed to be going blind from the slop they served, so we took our chance on their refreshments and were soon enjoying the effect. But we were not drunk like an Air Corps sergeant at the next table, who hap-

pened to see the cloth bar sewn on my fatigues indicating I was a lieutenant. He said something to me. I didn't get it. It was a slimy remark
about officers, which should have riled me, gotten me to fight, but I
wouldn't have cared had I heard. I was happily enjoying a nice buzz. Our
driver, a nice kid from the Bible Belt who didn't drink, smoke, or swear,
did hear. He grabbed the sergeant by the shirt, pulled him around so their
faces were three inches apart, and with his cherubic face looking ridicu-
lously angry, yelled, "You can't call one of our officers that!" Then he
let go with a right hook, sending the totally surprised sergeant sprawling
across his table, knocking over all the drinks on the way. With that, their
table started a fight with ours, and soon other tables joined in. It was
wonderful, just like a fight scene in a Wild West saloon from a
Hollywood movie. We broke away from the fight we had started and left
quietly, leaving the poor owner, hands wringing, running around plead-
ing for people to leave. There were fun times in the Army, and this was
one of them.

Lulls in combat were a time to clean weapons and ourselves — if it
rained, we might soap up and have a rain shower. Once, after a week
with no opportunity to even take my shoes off, my chance came. I threw
off my clothes; my body was filthy. Then I pulled off my shoes, wondering if I could stand the stink. Surprisingly, despite walking though
mud and though streams, my feet were amazingly clean — thanks to
heavy Australian wool socks that seemed to wick away grime and sweat.
Heavy shoes and heavy socks for hard use, I learned, are the way to have
healthy feet.

On quiet days — not quiet enough to remove shoes, but quiet enough
to sit at the edge of our foxholes ready to fight in case something happened — some would shave using their helmets as a bowl, some would
clean their rifles, some might just try to relax. These were times we
might talk. Sometimes I would prevail on Sergeant Johnson to sing a few
songs. He had a nice voice and would sing about life along the Ohio
River where he had his farm. Quiet times were joke-telling times. One
of my favorites involved two women who went to get their pictures
taken. The photographer seated them, then went to his camera and
pulled the cloth attached to the camera over his head.

First lady: "What's he gonna do under that cloth?"

Second lady: "He's gonna focus."
First lady, eyes now wide open in astonishment: "Both of us?"

Surely you laughed. I was laughing so hard I didn't hear the fellow shouting at me to report to Battalion headquarters.

Instead of receiving orders, I was handed a stack of money and told to pay the troops. A payroll? Here? We were nowhere. The enemy might open fire at any minute. Crazy. There was no place to buy anything, not even a flat place to shoot craps. Nevertheless, it was payday, and come hell or high water, the troops had to be paid. So off I went from foxhole to foxhole handing the soldiers pesos, the Philippine currency. I suppose it made sense to be paid in that currency. Occasionally we came across a village or a farm where we could buy a chicken or some eggs, but we could have bought any of these things by bartering our rations. Yet, old-timers from the New Guinea campaign confirmed that this was "normal," for there in the middle of the jungle, they had been paid in Dutch guilders, with absolutely no place to spend them, not even a nearby native village where there might be a native to sell a shrunken head.

But my view of the war was too narrow. We in the Infantry and the handful of medics, artillerymen, and engineers who shared the battlefield with us were but a fraction of the total Armed Forces. That we didn't have a place to spend our money, or a flat surface for shooting craps, didn't mean that others didn't. In the cities, in the villages, and in the barrios far back from the fighting, opportunities abounded for spending pesos. The thousands of soldiers staffing the hospitals, handling supplies, driving trucks, establishing phone lines and radio communication, repairing equipment, and doing all the hundreds of other things necessary to keep an army going had no problem finding places to spend their money. Whiskey was almost nonexistent but the bars overcame that handicap. Alcohol, often stolen from Army hospitals, could be colored to look like whiskey. So could wood alcohol. Either way, it sold well. The latter took its toll. On the way to Manila the Army erected a large sign that displayed a graph indicating the number of soldiers that had gone blind from drinking bad booze. There was no shortage of girls willing to give amatory satisfaction for a modest price, and gaming, gambling, and cock fighting were available. With pesos, service troops could lead a civilized life.

Soldiers in units out of range of gunfire lived a comfortable life, as I was to discover. When an SOS came through from a nervous captain of a quartermaster unit who suspected the presence of Japanese soldiers near his mess, two soldiers and I were sent to check it out. Reporting to the quartermaster, I was kept cooling my heels while he and his first sergeant argued about what kind of ice cream to have for dinner. The men were sick of chocolate every night and wanted maple walnut, even vanilla, anything for a change, but the captain argued for chocolate. Obviously, the captain was a wimp. If we had ice cream and Dick Fleming, our Company Commander, wanted chocolate, by God we would have had chocolate. But I can't imagine Dick bothering himself with anything as civilized as ice cream. Beer would have been another matter.

Dick was a good officer — but a wild man of sorts, who came by it naturally. He was a high school football hero. In his biggest game, the score was seven to six in his favor, with 30 seconds left, the opposing team with the ball, and the crowd going crazy. The quarterback dropped to pass, the intended receiver was in the clear. He got it. Touchdown! Not quite. From the first row of the stands where he had been watching the game, Dick's father leaped onto the field and tackled the receiver. Like father, like son. Dick would be anywhere he wanted to be and do what he wanted to do and the hell with the Japs. He was out to beat them. What I never could understand, however, was how he played football. He was so damned skinny. But he was wiry, and he had guts.

Dick talked constantly about his wife, Polly, back in the States, yet, if I can believe him, he never once wrote her a letter. She wrote him often, at least weekly. It was none of my business, but it used to drive me nuts thinking of the poor woman back home worried about her husband, never hearing from him. It was worry enough that he was an Infantry captain, but to never hear from him — it had to be torture. Yet Dick was not without heart or sentimentality. Tom Atchley told me that Dick once had to order him to take his platoon on a mission from which he had a good chance of not coming back. Dick was having a difficult time giving the order that probably meant sending men to their death. Dick didn't make it all the way; he couldn't hold back his tears.

I doubt that Major Mueller knew I had been sent to provide security for a quartermaster outfit. They were soldiers. They could provide their own security. And God help the quartermaster captain if Mueller knew he was so busy fretting about ice cream that he couldn't check on the presence of the Japanese himself. When Mueller was appointed Battalion Commander, an officer from Battalion headquarters came to him to ask which company was going to furnish security for the Command Post. The conversation as related to me was typically Mueller.

"Do your people in headquarters have weapons?" Mueller asked.

"Yes, sir, M1s and carbines."

"How about grenade launchers and bazookas?"

"They are back with the trains."

"Gathering rust, no doubt. Bring them up and be sure your soldiers know how to operate them. What about ammo? Do you carry the basic load?"

"I don't know, sir."

"Alright. See to it that headquarters soldiers are fully equipped with the right kind of weapons and supplied with the basic load of ammo. From now on this headquarters supplies its own security."

"But, sir, if the men have to provide security all night, they will be too tired to perform their own duties properly."

"Who provides securities for the rifle companies after they have been attacking all day?"

"They do, sir."

"You bet, and they have to attack again the next day. Being tired is a way of life on the battlefield and everybody in this Battalion has to share in this tiredness. You will provide security for the Command Post. Also, when you select the site, it is best to snuggle up to a front line company. Keeps us in better touch with the situation. Questions?"

"No, sir."

But I was hardly the one to sneer at the quartermaster. I had something of a chip on my shoulder. I was the combat soldier — tough, giving my all — and what the hell was this quartermaster doing for his country but fussing about ice cream. A chip, at best, doesn't earn anyone points, and I hadn't even earned the right for much of a chip having been in combat only about 30 days. Furthermore, I had spent most of the war in Denver living the country club life. At parties we had feasted on venison steak that tasted like choice beef right out of some quartermaster locker. While I was living it up in the lap of luxury, most of the soldiers in the Philippines — whether infantrymen lying in some trench

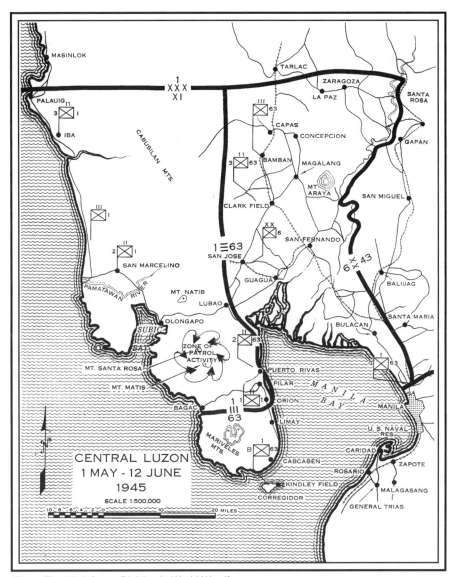

(From *The 6th Infantry Division in World War II*)

exposed to the elements, or truck drivers working through the night to deliver ammunition, or nurses in hot hospitals working around the clock to save lives — had been swatting mosquitoes and fighting malaria, all had had their share of slogging through mud, and most had done it in tropical New Guinea as well as the Philippines. Those who could get a little ice cream now and then deserved it. I had no right to complain. The quartermaster finally decided they would have strawberry.

As for the Japs, some had been reported in the area. We had heard of similar reports elsewhere. Our engineers had seen two emaciated-looking Japanese sitting unarmed 50 yards away across a stream from them, looking over in awe as bulldozer operators scraped out a road through what had been a tangle of vegetation and streambed of boulders. These were probably the kinds of Japs that had raided the quartermaster's garbage and had been upsetting his routines. We departed in disgust without making a search, hoping any leftover strawberry ice cream in the garbage cans wouldn't be too soupy for some starving Jap to enjoy.

And we, too, of the 3rd Platoon were to have a taste of civilization. Somewhere along the road between Manila and the great U.S. submarine base at Subic Bay lay the village of Guagua, pronounced like two frogs croaking almost simultaneously. Near Guagua, or perhaps from within the town itself, a small contingent of Japs were harassing traffic on this vital road. We were sent to clean them out of Guagua and off the roads.

With machine-guns mounted on jeeps, with hand grenades and ammunition hanging at our belts, with rifles at the ready, and with uniforms filthy from the mud of the slit trenches that were our homes, we roared into Guagua, slammed on the brakes, and jumped from our vehicles. If we had burst in on nuns at evening prayer, we couldn't have looked more foolish. Instead of a town suffering from oppression, we had bounded into a serene and prosperous community — handsome, well dressed, and lazily going about their business or simply enjoying a beautiful sunny day gossiping and visiting in the town square.

Like the fairy tale about the handsome prince trapped in the body of a frog, the town's name belied its loveliness. Instead of the usual bamboo and sheet metal huts that gave Philippine towns a flimsy and junky look, most buildings were a Spanish-style stucco. The town square was enhanced by a tiny white chapel at one end, really more of an enclosed altar than a church. Guagua, tidy and prosperous, despite the years of Japanese occupation and recent fighting that had devastated so many villages, was a peaceful oasis in a war-torn country.

From shops, from prosperous-looking homes, from the town square where people had been sitting and talking, the handsome people of Spanish and Philippine descent came forward to greet us. My eye fell on a beautiful young Eurasian girl, then on another, and another. Soldiers' eyes were popping out of their sockets. Here was trouble. Better for these people to contend with a few stray Japanese than a contingent of American soldiers who hadn't seen a woman for weeks, save for a few old crones scrounging in the fields for roots. But we had no trouble. The town took the soldiers to their hearts. And some to their beds.

It was May, in the Philippines a time for fiesta and festivals, for the celebration of Flores de Mayo, where, throughout the country, processions in honor of the Virgin Mary take place in the afternoon and evening. Young girls, the most beautiful in the villages dressed in white, decorate statues of Mary with flowers. Guagua was astir with preparations for their procession to honor the Virgin. On the street that ran between the church at one end of town to the chapel in the square at the other, garlands were being mounted on poles to mark the way for a procession to carry the Virgin's statue from the church to the chapel where it would be displayed for the month. On the day of the great event, a clear, warm, sunny day, elders carried the Virgin's icon on a platform bedecked with roses; young veiled women in flowing white dresses followed, each carrying a bridal bouquet as symbolic virginal brides of Jesus. I found the procession solemnly inspiring, yet festive. Here and there a bride discreetly turned her head to catch the eye of a soldier, bringing a smile to each.

All was going well, and then I saw him. My artless soldier, who had advised me of my men's oddly "impersonal" decision to kill me, was in the parade walking with the brides, his eyes downcast and looking as solemn as the most pious virgins. The good-hearted private would never have done anything to offend anyone, he just didn't realize how inappropriate his behavior. But I had to admit that he looked like he belonged in the parade. Seeing him amongst the virgins reminded me of a painting that I had over my bed when I was a child that portrayed Saint John as a curly-haired angelic child. And that was our soldier, curly headed, golden-haired, and angelic. Others seemed to be affected by him as I was, and instead of being offended, the town took to him. Thereafter, it seemed everyone was inviting this simple yet delightful lad to their homes.

But during our stay in Guagua, the normally conscientious and energetic private began to slip until he was practically a useless soldier. Claiming to be constantly tired, and looking drawn, I eased his duties, thinking he was out of sorts. The men knew what I didn't. The private had lost his virginity in Guagua and from there on had had a feast. He developed a following among certain girls who wanted to get to know this cute soldier. It was the consensus that it would take him a week to recuperate from his extra-curricular activities, once we would leave the town.

Until that time, the Guaguaions made us feel at home. Next door to the school where we were billeted, preparations were under way for a pig roast at the home of the town's wealthiest citizen. Decorations were going up, their well-tended yard was getting manicured, and fresh paint or whitewash was being applied to the house. Happily, one of their servants delivered a written invitation for me to attend. This was an affair I did not want to miss. I yearned for something civilized.

In the drive was a 1941 Chevrolet in new condition. Obviously, the prewar car had not been confiscated by the Japs. Granted, during the war, the Filipinos could have hidden some of their possessions, and if they had been kicked out of their homes they could have reclaimed them when the Japs left. But hide a car and keep it in perfect condition? Something wasn't right. If these people were collaborators, it wouldn't do for an American officer to attend their party. And so I watched the affair from the school with my tongue hanging out.

We essentially behaved ourselves in Guagua, except for one problem involving the military police. A certain squad leader in my platoon was a great soldier, but God help anyone and everyone if he got drunk — and drunk he got. Responding to a call from the MPs, I arrived at the town square. There in the middle was the soldier reeling, pistol in hand, the square deserted, the people having taken to the side streets. An MP poked his head around a corner. "Ha," the soldier shouted with glee and fired his pistol at him, knocking plaster off the corner of a building. While the drunken man was firing at this MP, another tried to sneak up from behind. "I know you're there you sonofabitch," he slurred as he wheeled around to fire at the second MP, who scurried for cover.

What to do? He was my soldier.

I called to him. He wheeled around and we faced each other. "I want your gun," I said, as I walked slowly toward him. There we were, the two of us facing each other in an otherwise deserted town square. Real Western shootout stuff. "I want your gun," I repeated.

"Nah," he mumbled, "I wanna get an MP. Sonza bitches." He fired a wild shot past me, again hitting a building where an MP had taken cover.

I kept walking toward him. "Give me the gun."

"Naw." Another wild shot. More fallen plaster.

When I was within three feet of him, he raised his gun to fire again.

"I told you I want your gun," I ordered.

"OK," he said and gave it to me.

Interestingly, this soldier later was a hero, and was found to have behaved admirably in a situation where he might have taken advantage of hard liquor. In Guagua I suspect he had been given some bad liquor that drove him wild. But even if he had gotten drunk on Beefeaters Gin, there isn't anyone who had been in combat as long as he who would have condemned him for getting drunk. Men can stand only so much, then they have to escape, some to institutions to hide in a dream world they will never leave. After a hangover, the soldier picked up where he had left off, a great soldier.

While in Guagua, for some reason long forgotten, I had to drive to Subic Bay and check in with an officer at the submarine base. Presumably I saw ships there, but I can't see them in my memory, nor can I conjure up an image of the harbor. As the home of our greatest Pacific naval base, I am sure there was much memorable to see. What I can recall through the fog of time was construction — earth-moving equipment at work rearranging the landscape, truckloads of giant timbers being hoisted in place to frame a building, carpenters swarming over the beams pounding away with hammers at a rate that sounded like machine-guns firing. Here were the legendary Seabees ("Construction Batallion") at work. Our own 6th Engineers were second to none in building bridges or clearing a road, but to compare our machinery to the Seabees at Subic Bay would be like comparing farm horses to giant air-conditioned combines. The Seabees' well-deserved can-do reputation was being put to use. In keeping with Navy priorities, they were building an Officers Club. Jealous as I was, I couldn't help admiring their work, especially the bar already completed and in business, a gorgeous structure made of Philippine mahogany at least a hundred feet long, all of it housed under a thatched roof, the sides open to the elements. The design was worthy of a first-class resort in modern Hawaii or the Caribbean. The best whiskeys were for sale cheap there, and my host, somewhat apologetically, let me know he was sensitive to the vast differences between the luxury at Subic Bay and the life I led. That said, he made sure I had a good time.

Chapter 12

Alphabet Soup

IPO DAM, downhill from Hell's Hill, was left to be taken by other Americans. Its enormity, its thick concrete walls, its setting in rugged hill country, its Japanese defenders — fanatics who would fight to the last man — made it impenetrable. How it could be attacked with anyone coming out alive was beyond comprehension. Even if an attack was successful, the Japanese could dynamite the dam and, if not destroy it, could easily ruin the valves and pipes that fed water to Manila, leaving the city in peril. Later, we heard that the dam had fallen intact with the loss of few, if any, Americans. The Air Corps bombed Ipo with napalm, a substance I had never heard of. Napalm, a fiercely burning liquid, was splattered over the dam and its fortifications, burning and suffocating the Japs and rendering them unable to carry out any mischief. Years later, during the Vietnam War, napalm became a symbol of American depravity, but I can't help wondering whether I owe my life to the stuff.

The line of Japanese defense in the area where we were concentrating our efforts was called the Shimbu Line, which suggested to me a line of trenches for each side, or at least some kind of definable battle front indicating we were here and they were there. Because I never perceived any kind of a line, and because the generals never took me into their confidence to give me the lay of the land, I went from battle to battle never quite figuring out what we were trying to accomplish except to kill Japs before they killed us. It's probably just as well I didn't know what we were up against.

General Tomoyuki Yamashita, the commander of the Japanese forces in the Philippines, had to realize that Japan had already lost the war, but what neither he nor the leaders of the United States knew was what the end would be like. The Japanese mind could neither conceive nor tolerate the notion of American invasion and occupation. And to lose the Emperor — he was practically a god. The United States had to be made to see that an invasion of Japan would be too costly. Therefore, Yamashita's best option was to hole up in strategic and defensible strongholds on Luzon where he could bleed us as much as possible, giving Japan a bargaining chip for ending the war on better terms. Under him he had three military groups to do the bleeding — one was the Shimbu Group, with 80,000 troops holed up in the mountains east of Manila under Lieutenant General Yokoyama. We, therefore, weren't fighting to push back a line; we were fighting in the mountains and the jungle to clean out his emplacements, from which he could harass the countryside, places often hidden until we walked into their fire. Hence the need for long-range patrols such as the one on my birthday where I had been sent to find and evaluate hidden defenses.

Yamashita's other military groups were the Shobu Group in northern Luzon, with 152,000 troops under Yamashita himself, and the 30,000-man Kembu Group under Major General Tsukada in the area around Clark Field. We would encounter these forces later, but for the moment we were getting our belly full from the Shimbu Group.

Mounts Pacawagan and Mataba, rising 1,400 feet above the Marikina Valley, were keystones in the Shimbu defense. The job of cutting off

Mount Pacawagan was given to the 145th Infantry and the Air Corps, Mount Mataba to us. Near Mataba's summit, three hills — A, B, and X — unimposing to look at, but laced with underground fortifications, were where the Japanese had hoped not only to make us bleed, but to hemorrhage. If these hills could be taken, the last of the two crutches on which the Japanese Shimbu forces were making their stand would be pulled out from under them. The 2nd Battalion of the 63rd had made its way up the mountainous areas to the base of A, B, and X, then from April 4th to the 7th had attacked A and X where they ran into intense fire from machine-guns, small-arms fire, knee mortars, and the big Japanese 150mm mortar. Suffering terrible casualties, the 2nd Battalion was withdrawn, and ours, the 3rd, was moved into place to take on the job.

Colonel Yon, Commander of the 63rd Infantry, agonized over our regiment's inability to take the hills. Direct orders had come from Division to concentrate on Hill A, considered the keystone in the Japanese defenses. Normally, Major Mueller and Colonel Yon, who were very close (Mueller called the Colonel "Dad," and Yon referred to Mueller as "Dutch"), would have worked out a battle plan together, but this time Yon ordered a direct assault. Mueller balked. He had other ideas for taking the hills. But Yon had no choice; the American 6th Army wanted to be done with the Japanese forces on the Shimbu Line. Pressure was on the 6th Division to take A, B, and X. Hill A was picked for the assault. The regiment had fooled around long enough trying to take it. It was time for an all-out assault no matter how bloody.

Knowing nothing of the strategic importance of Hill A, nor of the decision to launch an attack, nor that Major Mueller thought such an attack was suicidal, my platoon and I were moved into position at the base of A, below what seemed to be a small hill which, in the words of Mueller, looked like a moonscape, having been pounded bare of vegetation by artillery and mortar fire from previous battles. Mueller suspected that the entire area was honeycombed with a tunnel system connecting fire positions. I have complained about my frustration in never knowing what was going on, of not knowing where I was and why I was there. This time it was just as well that I didn't know. Of all the places to be in the Philippines, I was in the worst.

Because I wasn't privy to the proposed battle plan, and did not find out until 45 years later, let me tell the story as I saw it then. Our Battalion under Major Mueller was moved into position to take Hills A, B, and X, our Company positioned in the area of Hill A. We understood that days before, Company E had charged A like the Aussies against the Turks at Gallipoli, with results as disastrous. Frontal attacks, however, were not the way Mueller operated, so it never occurred to us that we might be in for such a thing. Japs on A, B, and X were just another tough football team for Mueller to beat. He hated war, but as long as he was in it he might as well enjoy the game. Should we charge the line, or do an end run? Deception was important. Whatever we did had to be unexpected. The only thing he couldn't do was forward pass. Helicopters were devices for future wars. Mueller, the football coach, was excited by the challenge. The enemy remained undefeated and no one had figured out how to beat them.

"What we will do," Mueller announced, "is charge them at night. They'll never expect it. We will go in with fixed bayonets, give them a taste of their own medicine."

Great! Just the thing for me. I'm the kind who stumbles over his own feet. The prospect of hand-to-hand fighting the Japs, who are weaned on the martial arts, spoiled my day. Mueller continued with the details. Silently, we were to crawl on our bellies up Hill A until we were virtually on top of the Japs, then charge them firing.

Inch by inch, up we crawled, higher and higher, undetected. We charged. Someone threw a phosphorus grenade, or possibly we tripped a Jap wire. Burning phosphorous fell around us but did little harm. What it did was add confusion to what, at best, was a confusing situation. Soldiers charged around not knowing whether the person coming at them was friend or foe. In the light of the burning phosphorous, I took a shot at someone coming at me. Whether I hit anyone I don't know — it was light for only a second. Anyway we weren't in a fight, we were in a melee. Mueller called off the attack. Lieutenant Wit of the 2nd Platoon, who had just come back to duty after weeks in the hospital recovering from a wound, was hit again, so it was back to the hospital. Several others were wounded, but my platoon came through OK. We would have to try again. Mueller was called to the meeting where he was told it was time to stop fooling around and take the hill with a frontal assault, but I knew nothing about that.

Europe's war was a war of tanks and self-propelled weapons; our war was more like the French and Indian wars in the 18th century. While those who had landed in Luzon before me had seen a small sample of armored warfare as they swept across the flat lands and chased the Japs into the mountains, I arrived to fight them in the mountains on terrain unsuitable for tank warfare. I had yet to see a tank or anything like one. But that was about to change. Mueller — I thought it was Mueller — got help from our engineers who cleared a way through the rugged terrain and succeeded in bringing up a self-propelled 8-inch howitzer, a short cannon that usually fires in a high trajectory over some distance. Instead of using it in traditional fashion, however, the cannon was placed as close to Hill A as possible so that it could fire short range — flat, like a rifle. At dawn, the plan called for my platoon to start crawling up the hill. I was to carry a radio with me so that I could call back when we were catching fire, pinpointing as best I could where it was coming from. At the site of the howitzer itself, and at other vantage points, observers were to train their binoculars on the hill, searching for enemy activity. With everyone feeding in observations, the howitzer was to be fired at suspected targets, even those only a few yards from us.

At night we moved to the very base of Hill A, which because of its size made me think of a small rise back home where the Red Jacket Ski Club had rigged up a rope tow powered by an old Buick motor — an odd thing to think of here in a tropical land. But A was an ugly little hill packed with misery. In the dark waiting for the dawn, I could make out our soldiers hunched over their rifles, eyes closed, trying to get a last-minute wink before dawn. The date was April 10. The first sign of light was strangely beautiful, strangely peaceful. In my mind I could hear the resonant voice of Lawrence Olivier speaking lines from Shakespeare's *Henry the Fifth:*

> Now entertain conjecture of a time
> When creeping murmur and the poring dark
> Fills the wide vessel of the universe.
> From camp to camp, through the foul womb of night,
> The hum of either army stilly sounds,
> That the fix'd sentinels almost receive
> The secret whispers of each other's watch.

Fire answers fire, and through the paly flames
Each battle sees the other's umber'd face.

We crawled up. Not much fire from Japs. But when they fired, one of us crawling up the hill, or a spotter back at the howitzer, would sense where the fire came from and relay the message back to the howitzer for it to do its job. Most of the time those of us crawling on the ground could pinpoint targets before the Japs fired. Miraculously we made it to the top without anyone getting hit. We were few, just a platoon, not enough of a force to withstand much of a counterattack. But the Japs were slow in launching it. We had time to dig in and to be reenforced. Possibly because we had succeeded where others had failed, the Japs must have thought we had attacked in greater numbers than before, hesitating to counterattack until they had assembled a sizeable force. Whatever they planned was sure to come, but it didn't come . . . and it didn't come. Just as we were feeling secure, it came. Not the scream of Japs charging up the hill to drive us off, but a scream that sounded like a giant sheet being ripped over our heads. Like a volcano erupting, earth was blown into the air showering us with dirt and dust. Smoke from a cigarette I had lit had been trailing upwards. When it hit, my smoke jumped to the side from the concussion, like a pin being hit by a bowling ball. Silence would follow — 20, 30, 40 seconds of silence — then the scream again. The Japs had brought up their 150mm mortars and were lobbing huge shells upon us, figuring they could either kill us or drive us off the hill with mortar fire.

In Russian roulette a revolver is placed to the head and the trigger is pulled — will it be just a harmless click or will it fire a fatal bullet? We were in a game of Japanese roulette. They would lob a mortar and its missile would come screaming straight down. To kill, it had to land directly in a foxhole, or at least within a few feet of it. Another scream as a mortar was about to land, another explosion — I thought I heard somebody exclaim, "Gracious!" Again it came, and again I heard, this time more clearly, "Bless my soul!" Again, and again, "Oh my goodness!" And after each hit, from a hole at the north end of our perimeter, from the mouth of our platoon's master of the art of the four-letter word, came, "Dearie me! Oh for heaven's sake!" I thought I heard someone crying, then I realized someone was laughing. As the "dearie me's" and the "gosh" and "gollies" continued, more guys started to laugh. The scene was crazy, the situation crazy. And we were laughing so hard the Japs could have walked over us.

So it went, and so we survived. Ammunition for their huge mortars must have been limited, because the shelling tapered off to an occasional lob from smaller mortars. More serious trouble came from small-arms fire. Sticking my head out of my hole, I heard a sharp snap like the crack of a whip telling me a sniper's bullet had come close to hitting me in the head. What the Japs couldn't do to kill us with heavy weapons they were now going to do with sniper fire. But no damn Jap was going to get a bead on me if I could help it. When I had to be out of my hole checking on the men, I sprang out like a jack-in-the-box. I ran, I zigged, I zagged, I bobbed, I stopped, I started, I did a Saint Vitus's dance.

Oh Jesus! A blond kid, one of the youngsters that had just joined us, was sitting beside his foxhole, not in it. I yelled at him to get down. He grinned. "Aw, Lieutenant," he said, "don't worry, when your number is up your number. . ." He never finished. A small round hole in the middle of his forehead oozed blood as he slumped over. Before the night was over, we lost two more replacements, just youngsters. Yet, for all its danger, sniper fire seemed like a relief compared to the heavy mortar fire. In some sense, the feeling was justified. When a mortar landed sending shrapnel in all directions, we had to stay below ground, but if we kept from making a good sniper's target by keeping on the move, we could work above ground to improve our defenses without much chance of being hit.

We were not alone on top of that hill for long. Our engineers showed up with a bulldozer to build a road up to us for delivering heavier weapons to turn the hill into a fortress; first for defense, then as a base for fire power to support our troops when they attacked the remaining hills. Enemy mortar fire began again to try to stop these reenforcements. Shrapnel hit the engineer supervising the road building, leaving his left side and arm a bloody mess. But I remember him talking calmly to his sergeant, giving instructions before he left for the battalion aid station. Overall, by the time it was over, taking A, B, and X cost us 27 dead and 127 wounded.

When it was safe to wander over Hill A without fear of being blown to bits, Father Dietz, the regimental chaplain, searched the area collecting remnants of men "missing in action," most from the Gallipoli-like attacks of those who tried to take the hill before us. In a cemetery somewhere, there is a proper grave for the men who died there. It reassured the men to know that should they too be killed, Father Dietz would see to it that they would rest in a marked grave, rather than lie ignominiously rotting on some distant battlefield.

Dietz endeared himself to the soldiers in many ways. I can still see this gaunt, stoop-shouldered Jesuit looking like a character right out of a Mauldin cartoon, bandoliers hanging all over him, bent over from his load of ammunition, coming along with us up the long trek 1,000 feet up from the valley to the base of Hills A, B, and X. If the trail had been wide enough for his jeep, he would have brought it up to say mass, using the hood for an altar. Under the rules of war, a clergyman had no business carrying those bandoliers, but carrying them endeared him to the soldiers. That he could carry as much as he did was quite the subject. "Guess how old he is?" someone would ask, then without waiting for a reply the answer would come: "He's forty!" With many of the original men of the regiment dating back to the days of the New Guinea operation now gone, young replacements probably brought the average age of the troops down to half the age of Dietz.

As it turned out it wasn't Major Mueller, as I had thought, who cooked up the plan that led to the capture of Hill A. The credit belonged to Dick Fleming, our Company Commander, and Major Bob Wells, the Battalion Executive Officer. Mueller was absent. After our failure to take the hill in a night attack, General Walter Krueger, 6th Army Commander, had called a conference of officers, including Mueller, to review the whole problem of Hill A. Here's what really happened, according to Mueller:

> I had gone to Division Command Post along with the other BN. [Battalion] Commanders to brief General Walter Krueger, the Sixth Army Commander, on how we were going to take Hills A, B, & X. My plan was simple. [Mueller drew a sketch on his letter showing a triangle, A and B points at the base, X at the top. K Company was to attack A, While L and I companies were to do an end run around to X and the 2nd Battalion of the 63rd hit B from the flank.]

I was severely criticized by an Assistant Division Commander of the 6th Division. He said that my plan was doomed to failure on two counts: 1) I needed to first capture Hill A to establish a base of fire and then attack Hill X; and 2) the 20th Infantry had said that the route of attack around Hill X was so rough that it was impassable for Infantry. My reply was that each of my Rifle Companies carried their own base of fire; and that K Company's attack would keep the enemy on Hill A occupied while we circled around it; and that the route to Hill X was not nearly as rough as the terrain at Objective New York which we had taken at the north flank of the Lingayen Gulf beachhead.

Then the Assistant Division Commander turned to General Hurdis, our Division Commander, and said, "General, it is your decision." General Hurdis paused, sucked on his pipe, and then said, "Well, it's the 63rd's mission; I'll let them do it the way they want to."

With that, General Krueger jumped up, shook hands with each one of us, and said, "God bless you and your troops."

When I approached our area from the Division briefing, much to my amazement, I saw soldiers walking around on top of Hill A. I knew damned well that they weren't Japs because only Americans were damned fools enough to expose themselves like that. So, my base of fire problem was solved by the initiative on the part of my illustrious comrades in arms. During the night, we loaded up Hill A with firepower. We put M Company machine-guns up there along with the .50 Cal machine-guns of our Z force. Our Z force was our cooks, mechanics, supply sergeants, and armorer-artificers. They were armed with at least six .50 Cal MGs, as far as I can recall. They loved to be able to participate in operations, whenever it was possible. And their machine-guns were always in good shape. (At the Agricultural School, in an earlier battle, they distinguished themselves by knocking out some armored personnel carriers after the Jap Armored Division broke through our front lines.)

The next morning, the battle for X was a piece of cake. We had one 8 in. Howitzer Bn, one 105 Bn and one 4.2 Mortar Company in support of our attack besides the two Cannon Company guns. At the same time, the Air Force smoked the more distant observation points.

I detailed Lt. Elmore of I Company, whose platoon was the right unit on our sweep around Hill A, to call off the artillery when it got too close. He had the most guts and I knew that he would keep the artillery going until the last moment, which is exactly what happened.

We took Hill X without incident because all of the Japs had their heads down. We, of course, had a reorganization plan. But the two Company Commanders were conscientiously trying to organize such a perfect defense of the terrain that I had to step in as a practical matter because I feared that the Jap 150 mortars would soon start to blast us. So, I stood in the middle of the force and yelled as loud as I could, "Everybody grab a shell hole and get in it, right now!" Which everybody did and not a moment too soon; the Jap 150s began to rain down on us.

About the same time, the M Company machine-gunners who had displaced to the north end of our position reported that they could see a Jap force moving in from the north along the ridge line to counter-attack us. I noted that those Japs were in an area covered by a pre-planned 8 inch protective barrage; so, I turned to my Artillery liaison officer who brought down devastating fire right smack on the Jap force. They disappeared and were not heard from again.

One interesting sequel to this attack was this. In mopping up we saw that there was a cave in the saddle between Hills A & B. We covered it with fire and somebody got close enough to throw several charges into the cave. We found the dead bodies of a number of Japs — seven Jap officers of whom one obviously was the Battalion Commander of the battalion that had been facing us. My guess is that he called an early morning meeting of his Company Commander to decide what to do about Hill A, which you and your heroes had taken the day

before. Our attack solved all of his problems for him forever.

So there you have it; the fine results of your seizure of Hill
A. I have used your seizure of Hill A in my absence many
times in lectures on initiative; now, at last, I know who led that
attack.

It is nice to learn that we had taken so important a Japanese defensive
position. My parents sent me an item from a Buffalo paper telling about
the battle and the fall of a key part of the Japanese defenses. I wrote my
parents that I had led the attack, thinking they would be pleased. It only
made them feel worse because it so graphically reminded them of the
danger I was in. My parents so disapproved of my joining the Infantry
that, then and forever after, they never said anything approving of what
I had done in the war.

Mueller's description of what happened in the saddle brings back two
memories that sometimes, even almost 50 years later, awaken me in the
middle of the night to give me a good case of anxiety. The first has to do
with the blowing up of the cave Mueller mentioned. We had been on Hill
A from dawn of the first day clear through the next, digging in, taking
shelling, dodging bullets, and getting no sleep. Nor did I have much
sleep the night before the attack. Furthermore, except for a greasy C
ration, which I couldn't eat because of heartburn (a plague all my life),
I hadn't eaten for almost two days. The worst of the battle over, a few of
us at a time were to go down to the field kitchen to get something to eat,
my turn last. On my way down, Dick Fleming hailed me saying he
wanted me to take some shape charges and blow up a cave. I don't know
what raced through my mind in that second, but I snapped at him and
told him I was part of the crew going to eat. Sometimes in the middle of
the night I awake wondering, did I really give a damn about eating?
Most of the time, eating was something I made myself do. Was I just trying to get out of a nasty job? Was I so bushed that I didn't give a damn
about anything? All I know is that when Mueller refers to us as heroes,
I don't feel much like a hero, especially when I think about passing that
job on to someone else. I can't get it out of my system that I was a coward that day. Ken Johnson and Tim Timmerman blew the cave, or caves
as it turned out. Thank God they came out alive. If they had died doing

a job I felt I should have done, my life would have been as worthless as Judas's 30 pieces of silver. Happily, these two great soldiers won Silver Stars for their effort.

The men who were in on this mission said that, as Mueller suspected, the holes were interconnected by tunnels. A charge dropped in one hole would send Japs flying out another. One of the men who provided cover for Johnson, a tall, soft-spoken Okie, dark-skinned, with a stubble of a black beard that made him look sad like Jesus on the cross, told me a Jap had stuck a sawed-off shotgun out of a hole at him. "They're illegal, aren't they, Lieutenant?" he asked in all sincerity. I didn't know, but asked what he did about it. "Why, I took it away from him and hit him over the head with it."

The other incident involved the saddle between A and B. We had been taking fire and I was sure it was coming from the saddle. I called for a round of mortar fire, which landed about a hundred yards from where I thought it should. I gave some corrections, but for some reason I didn't get what I wanted. And probably for good reason. One of our patrols might have been operating in the area where I wanted fire and I wouldn't have known about it. But I wasn't thinking of the bigger picture, just my own little perimeter on Hill A. Anyway, not getting what I wanted, I decided to work my way over the edge of our perimeter toward the saddle and get a better look. Finding nothing, I moved further, then still further until I realized I might even have reached Hill B, still in enemy hands. It was high time, and then some, to get back. Then it happened. Overhead, I heard what sounded like a freight train rolling across the sky — probably, I thought, one of our artillery shells headed for an enemy target. It smashed near me. All of a sudden it was Hell's Hill all over again, except I couldn't figure out where the fire was coming from or who was firing: the Japs at me, or Americans at Japs? I was, after all, in enemy territory.

A nearby boulder offered protection. I made for it and crouched down, anticipating my fate. Instead of being scared, my life began to pass before me — my wonderful parents, my happy childhood, the girl I had hoped to marry. If I had to go, I was ready to go peacefully. I thanked God for a good life.

Let every man in mankind's frailty

> Consider his last day; and let none
> Presume on his good fortune
> until he finds
> Life at his death, a memory without pain
>
> Shakespeare's *Oedipus Rex*

Miraculously, the firing shifted away from me. If it was fire from the Japs, perhaps they thought they had finished me off. I made it back to the platoon.

Strangely, until reading Mueller's letter, I had never looked back at that experience with any sense of anxiety over what might have happened. What bothers me now is my stupidity. Mueller had orchestrated a battle. Like a fool I started to play another tune without checking to see if it fit in with his plan. From reading Mueller's letter and from reading a history of the 6th Division, I now believe I participated in the final battle for A, B, and X from the wrong side of the fence.

Chapter 13

Engine Trouble and Salt Pills

WITH THE JOB at A, B, and X completed — or as the papers put it, "The vaunted Shimbu Line having been cracked . . ." — we moved on to an area about ten miles north of Clark Field in May, in central Luzon, ostensibly to ferret out stray Japs, an easy task, a cross between rest and combat. Mostly we rested. We refurbished equipment, ate, slept (on a real canvas cot in a tent), and played games. I found myself getting boxing gloves slipped over my hands and being pushed into a ring to box with one of the men in the company. At Cornell I was student manager of boxing so I knew something about the sport and did pretty well until my opponent connected. After that I thought I was swimming. I wish I could have done better, but I had a good time and so did the men, especially when they saw me reeling. During these "rests," Dick Fleming would get a game of poker going. Others would get another kind of a game going with a nearby Filipino woman. When it came time to leave encampments like this, there would always be girls hanging around, laughing and waving us on, save an occasional weeping one hanging on to a tailgate, trying to stop a truck from carrying off the man who was the father of her unborn child.

Give soldiers ten minutes in one place and they will build things — chairs, a table, shelters, all kinds of things — and always a platform and a barrel for water with holes in it for a shower, something as it turned out we didn't need in the Clark Field area. Frequent rains made the sky our shower. As we showered naked, we were watched by naked people. We were in the land of the Negritoes, delightful little people about four feet tall. While we reveled in the rain, they shielded themselves with large leaves found in the nearby mountain forest.

Negritoes were forever coming up with rumors of stray Japs prowling around their villages. Chasing these rumors got me to some of their villages where I hoped to see something exotic, possibly a native dance or a tribal ceremony, or at the least quaint grass huts, but all I ever saw were people staring at me from old crates and similar junk that provided them shelter. I had come to see the natives, but I think we had been lured to their villages so that the natives could see the unbelievably ugly-looking white giants.

A more substantial rumor led to a chase up a long defile in the mountains. By jeep, four of us worked our way six or so miles up a road — or more accurately a trail — until we came to a spot where there had obviously been some kind of an encampment. Lying about were items such as a Japanese bayonet and a leather case. I still have the case. Disembarking, rifles at the ready, we spread out and poked into the forest no more than 25 yards or so, but deep enough in that dense vegetation to lose sight of our jeep. Returning to the vehicle, we found a poncho missing. Obviously we were being watched, and the only way we could locate the Japs in that thick foliage was for them to fire on us. In my mind, and undoubtedly in the minds of the Japs, it was a no-win situation for either of us to start a fight.

We jumped into the jeep, switched on the ignition, and stepped on the starter. The starter ground away. No sign of ignition. The driver tried again. No luck. The Japs must have screwed up the engine. They had us just where they wanted us. One more try with the starter. She sputtered, then caught hold. Off we went. Life in the service had its moments.

It was during this period at Clark Field that I may have been sent to Guagua because friends at reunions have told stories of our stay that I do not remember. Joe E. Brown, the famous comedian, visited Clark Field and put on a show. Major Mueller was promoted to lieutenant colonel, and as the story goes, Joe E. Brown pinned on his silver oak leaf.

Peace and quiet never lasted long. In July 1945, the Cordilleras lay ahead, mean mountains in Central Luzon characterized by high peaks, deep rocky gorges, raging streams fed by constant rains, narrow steep roads, and vegetation so thick an armored vehicle painted like a bright red fire truck could have been hidden from view three feet off a road — every terrain feature to work in favor of the the defender of the Cordilleras, General Yamashita, known infamously in his previous assignment as the "Tiger of Malaya." The Cordilleras had everything and more that General Yamashita needed to make it miserable for us who were determined to make it his last stand.

Initially in the Cordilleras campaign we were to move the one lousy mile from the village of Bolog to the village of Kiangan on Highway 4 and Old Highway 4. I took 11 days from July 1 to 12 to do it; 250 yards the first day and 250 the next, then four more days to cover the next 1,500 yards. After that we faced a narrow 25 yards of road sandwiched between a cliff on one side and thick brush on the other. We made it through in a day, and after that we really picked up speed, moving several hundred yards for a couple of days thanks to less dense brush and not-so-steep cliffs and gulches. And so it went, creeping ahead one day, slow but steady the next, one company moving down the road, another clearing out to the sides, a company from the rear moving through the lead company to take over the lead, and so on to Kiangan.

And after Kiangan? Move on. More of the same. Tedious days, cautious days, rainy days, sleepless days, filthy days, the job to be done was a stinking job, but we were killing and not being killed. Much of the

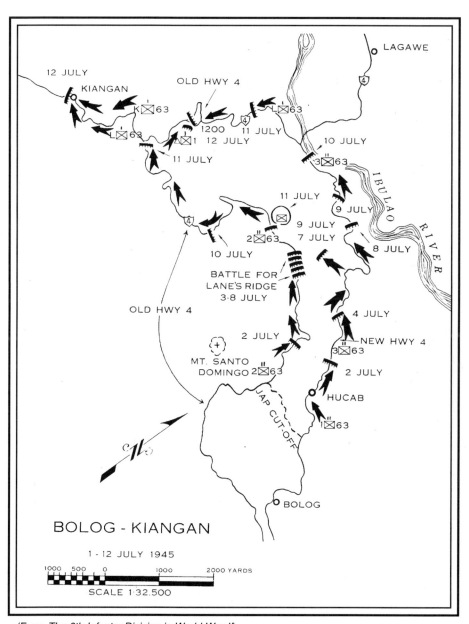

(From *The 6th Infantry Division in World War II*)

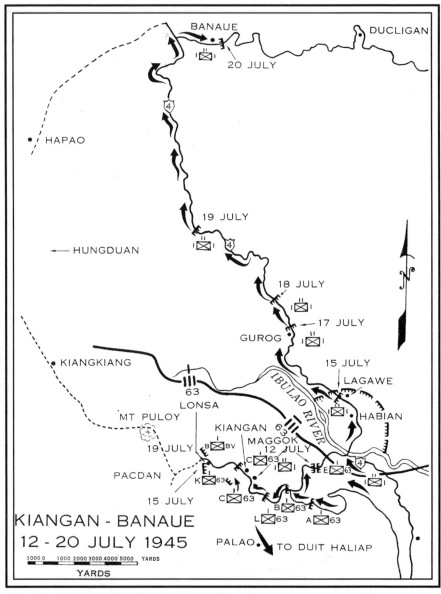

KIANGAN - BANAUE
12 - 20 JULY 1945

(From *The 6th Infantry Division in World War II*)

credit for our luck was probably due to the Air Corps that regularly strafed suspected Japanese positions. While making our way along a bad stretch, one of our planes flew low, firing a few feet to the side of us, pumping .50-caliber bullets into the the dreaded Jap-infested brush. We cheered. But was this an intended favor? Later on when I was in the hospital, a plane spotted my outfit and, thinking them Japanese, raked them with machine-gun fire. When its .50-caliber bullets struck a soldier in his rump, meat flew off like it had been hit with a sledgehammer, according to the men who saw it. Did the pilot who strafed the roadside a few feet from us think we were Japs and was just a lousy shot? In any event, the risk of being hit by friendly fire was worth it. Getting through that terrain would have been far bloodier without planes to rake fire into the brush.

Day by day, inch by inch, rain or shine, we worked our way up that winding dirt road known as Old Highway 4. Raging water from all the rain swept away the bridge over the Ibulao River we had recently crossed. It's a sickening feeling to see water on the rampage tearing apart everything in its way. It's a sickening feeling to be a thin line of men with no chance to retreat across the river to main forces should the enemy attack with overwhelming strength. It's a sickening feeling knowing that ammunition, food, and medicine can't be brought to you. It's a sickening feeling knowing you can't be gotten out to a hospital if wounded. But leave it to the engineers. Anchoring six captured Japanese trucks at intervals across the stream, they laid planks across the truck bodies to create a bridge. This was the situation Mueller later told me about. Later on, when the men faced a raging stream and tried to cross it by gripping each in a human chain, they couldn't hold. Several were swept to their death. I missed this because I was in the hospital, but I also missed getting into the land of the hanging rice paddies of the Philippines, considered by many to be one of the wonders of the world. When I returned from the hospital it seemed that every other soldier couldn't wait to tell me about this unbelievable and wonderful sight. Our Division had been known as the *Sightseers* from its days in the First World War, when it was moved around in France like a pawn in chess that never gets involved in any important action. Now the Division was seeing many sights and fighting every step of the way to see them.

When a platoon took the lead up the road, say about 50 yards ahead

Kiangan area terrain. (From *The 6th Infantry Division in World War II*)

of the rest of the company, its leader might want to relay tactical information to his company commander and do it from a position of cover without shouting. To make it possible to talk softly so as not to be heard by the enemy while taking cover hiding behind a tree or crouching beside a hillock, Infantry companies had radio phones known as walkie-talkies, devices about the size and shape of a quart milk carton. More often than not communicating with these devices went about like this:

> "I can't hear you, talk louder. What? You think there's a machine-gun nest?"

The 6th Engineers bridge the raging Ibulao River by anchoring captured Japanese trucks and laying planking across the truck bodies. (From *The 6th Infantry Division in World War II*)

"No, I said I see a sniper to your west."
"Oh, you want a rest."

The best thing to do was to put the damn thing down, stand out in the open where you could see who you wanted to talk to, and shout. My grandchildren have toy walkie-talkies. They cost about $20 for the set. They are about one-third the size and weight of those we used. They transmit ten times farther, and are many times more reliable.

At night we set up defense perimeters with machine-guns placed for crossfire, riflemen in slit trenches in between, and trip wires attached to flares to light the area and expose any enemy that might penetrate our area. About two o'clock one morning flares went up. In short order, 12 Japs made the supreme sacrifice for their emperor. They went down in a clatter that sounded like knives, forks, and spoons being thrown about. In the morning I saw a sight that took me back to my medical days, to my days in the operating room as a surgical technician, to my friends who were now running a hospital in Europe. Hemostats, retractors, knives, scissors — beautiful instruments by the way — were scattered everywhere. A medical unit had marched into our trap. In the pocket of one of the dead Japs, a kid no more than 15, was a wallet with a picture of him in his uniform standing ever so proudly with his parents, simple people, probably farmers judging from the house and farm tools in the background. This lad lying dead in the road was no cruel brute. He was a human being. I felt sick.

As it happened, I was sick, but I didn't know it. At best, none of us were ever healthy. Nobody ate much. When I joined Company K, I would scavenge food the men didn't eat; a cookie perhaps, their mixed canned fruit, and always their chocolate bar, a real jaw breaker made hard so that it wouldn't melt in the heat. "Give yourself a month," the veterans said, "and you won't eat either." In three weeks I stopped eating the chocolate. Three weeks later I ate just to stay alive. Most repulsive was the Coca-Cola, made by mixing syrup with warm water. No carbonation. It's been 47 years since I have had a Coke. If I live 40 more, I don't think I could get one down. When I see kids drinking it, especially with their meal, I feel queasy. However, I ate lots of crackers with jelly, and they remained a favorite. But it was almost impossible to get one in my mouth before the flies landed on the jelly and stuck to it, giving us a source of protein as well as calories. We carried our own flies. We didn't have to wait for them to come over from the piles of excrement, which is where they get their protein. They could get it from us by eating away at sores on the back of our hands: "jungle rot," we called it.

Salt was my problem, according to my own diagnosis. The body has to have a certain amount of salt. I sweated mine out. Each day I had less and less strength, no longer enough to dig a slit trench to be in at night for protection. Each day I would ask that salt pills be sent up with the rations. None came. My urine began to get red, soon dark red like Coca-Cola syrup. One night machine-guns opened up. Ours? Theirs? The Filipinos who had latched on to fight with us? They were apt to be trigger happy. Bullets were flying everywhere, and I was lying above ground. I was angry. If I didn't get some salt pills and get back my strength, I'd be done in. In the morning I took off for the field kitchen to demand salt pills. The Battalion surgeon happened to be there drinking a cup of coffee. Hearing me bitch, he came over and took one look at my jaundiced skin and especially my eyes. I had no whites left. They were a dark yellowish brown. Hepatitis, the scourge of the Army, caught me. "Lieutenant," he said, "you don't need salt pills. There's an ambulance at the aid station. Go down and get in it."

Somehow, in those rugged mountains, Filipinos managed to carve a few flat places into the mountainside for rice paddies. One was converted to an air field capable of handling a Norduyn Norseman, a large single-engine transport, built by the Canadians for landing and taking off in difficult places, ideal for carrying out the ill and wounded. Four companions — they wounded and I ill — were transferred to the Norseman and flown to a hospital at Rosario in Central Luzon, where I underwent a series of blood transfusions to cure my hepatitis — a treatment, the brainstorm of one of the doctors who felt this was a way to get soldiers back into action quickly, that proved to be as effective as giving a quick charge to a dead battery.

So it was back in action for me. But in less than a week I was no better able to soldier than before, so back to the "airport," now enlarged to handle the C-47 Skytrain, the military equivalent of the civilian Douglas DC-3, the famous two-motor workhorse plane of World War II, rigged in this case as an ambulance to handle a dozen patients. Two of the ambulance planes were on the runway, one ready to take off, the second

Manila, April 1945.

waiting. I was in the second. The first, revved up but held back by her brakes, was finally released to let her go. Off she tore down the runway. She wasn't going to make it. The pilot slammed on the brakes, but not soon enough. She flipped into the ditch at the end of the runway. That

Manila, April 1945.

plane dragged out of the way, our turn came. Our pilot came back into the cabin to look over his cargo. He saw a couple of men on stretchers, then he looked at me. "Can you walk?" he asked, then without waiting for an answer he made a general announcement: "All of you who can walk come forward and lean against the bulkhead between the cabin and crew." Engines were revved until the plane was about to shake apart, but the pilot held her back. It didn't seem the brakes alone could have held her. She must have been tethered. An axe must have cut it. Suddenly, like a tightly wound spring being let go, we shot forward. Off we went into the wild blue yonder, once again headed for Rosario.

For me, the war was over, but I didn't know it. I'd get well, I thought. Or well enough. I'd get back to my outfit. They might still be working their way up Old Highway 4. If not that highway, another highway, another hill. There weren't many Japs left to be killed in the Philippines. Japan would come next. The Japanese would fight to the last man to keep us from landing, but we would land. I might make it through. I might not. The worst would be after we landed. Every inch would be blocked by a Jap, some dug in holes, others fortified in concrete bunkers yards thick, others fighting from buildings, others from trees. They would never give up. They would all die, one by one. We had seen that in the Philippines. By 1949 it would be over. Four more years. Millions would be dead. Odds for survival were nil. Only a severe wound taking me out of action would help to beat the odds. I didn't think about that. I didn't think about much. I was on automatic pilot. No more thoughts about romance, no more thoughts about a great adventure, no more thoughts about having stories to tell my grandchildren, just a mind set on keeping on going, on doing my best to finish the job.

I had, however, a hope. In February, at a casual station I met a physician on his way back to the United States who had been a prisoner of the Japanese. He talked about his Japanese guards and how their attitudes changed from arrogance to bravado when American planes flew over their camp. "When Germany falls," he said, "Japan will say, 'Germany let us down. We can't fight the whole world by ourselves. We will have to give up.' That will be their out, their way to save face." Maybe so, but by that time Germany had capitulated a good two months before, and the Japanese were still fighting like trapped rats.

This time in the hospital I did nothing except sleep and eat sour balls. That and shower, which got me out of bed and gave me a chance to talk to other patients. If I stayed in bed I would promptly fall asleep. At the showers, mostly we talked about the nurses, but talk of something big happening began to creep into the conversation. A friend had a friend in the Air Corps who told him something was up. One guy wanted to bet on the end of the war, but there were no takers. Then we heard that an atomic bomb had been dropped, the wonderful atomic bomb that saved our lives. Hope. Reprieve. Life took on an entirely different meaning. There might be a future. It would have been very difficult to go back and fight now knowing it might be over. I don't see how our soldiers in Vietnam fought knowing that on a certain date, July 10 or August 15, for example, their enlistment would be up and they could go home. That, I should imagine, would concentrate the mind on saving one's rear instead of finishing the job.

Forever, we will argue that Japan was ready to surrender, that the bomb was unnecessary. That question should and does bother our national conscience. Statesmen in Japan knew the war had to end, but as Suburo Ienaga, a leading Japanese scholar, wrote in *The Pacific War:*

> . . . the military were as dangerous as they were ridiculous. Refusing to surrender, they demanded a great battle to bloody the Allies on the beaches, drive off the invaders, and gain better terms. The military saw the Allied approach as the "golden opportunity," as the "divine chance" they had been waiting for. Faced with such obstinate opponents, the senior statesmen had to be extremely careful. The army might assassinate peace advocates or stage a coup d'etat. Real intentions screened by secrecy, Jushin [*the cabinet ministers and other political advisers*] maneuvered delicately toward ending the war.

Without the bomb as the ultimate argument, the peace faction may never have gotten its way. And most of us in Company K would have died.

Luck had been with me. My decision to join the Infantry had paid off. I had caught the war near the end. I spent only five months in hell. The campaign in Luzon was against a beaten enemy holed up in the mountains with but one aim, to bleed us so badly that America might have second thoughts about invading Japan. The Japanese lacked the weapons to throw tons of explosives at us. I participated in nothing like the landings in Normandy, but what I did see was jungle fighting, fighting that required stealth, patrolling, and smart and courageous men disciplined to work as a team. My great fortune was to serve under a great battalion commander who brought out the best in these men, who used them in clever and unusual ways to outsmart and outwit a smart and treacherous enemy. Most treasured is my memory of the men, most of them from rural areas in the Dakotas, Minnesota, and the states bordering on the Mississippi down as far as Arkansas. They were farmers, mechanics, shopkeepers — independent cusses all. How to describe them?

In a single hour after supper on the evening of the 22nd of February 1899, cracker-barrel philosopher Elbert Hubbard wrote the short story, "A Message to Garcia" for his magazine, *The Philistine,* as it was about to go to press at his institute in East Aurora, New York. In a way, what he wrote expressed what I am trying to say. His essay was about a Lieutenant Rowan, an officer in the war between Spain and the United States. President McKinley needed to send a message to Garcia, the leader of the insurgents in Cuba. No one knew the location of Garcia's hideout in the mountains of Cuba. What to do? Someone said to the President, "There is a fellow by the name of Rowan who will find Garcia if anyone can." Rowan took the message and delivered it to Garcia. He didn't ask, "Where is he at? Who is Garcia?" He simply took the message and delivered it.

Hubbard's story in praise of a man who had a job to do and did it, of a man who never said, "Why me?" or "It isn't my job," stirred the world. It caught the eye of the president of the New York Central Railroad, who reprinted a half a million copies for his customers. Prince Hilakoff of the Russian Railways saw the article and had it translated and given to every one of his employees. During the Russo-Japanese war of 1904-1905, copies were made for Russian soldiers. Some fell into the hands of the Japanese. On the order of the Mikado, every man in the employ of the Japanese government, soldier or civilian, was given a copy. Over 40 million copies of "A Message to Garcia" have been printed. Over 40 million copies of an essay in praise of a man who had the backbone, the courage, and the willingness to take on a job and do it.

Dick Fleming was a Rowan. So was Ken Johnson, Tim Timmerman, Tom Atchley, Rufus Bryant, Charles Lanham — Company K was a company of Rowans. We were often short of men, but never of Rowans. Toward the end of the war the men coming in as replacements were just

Left to right: Lieutenants Munschauer, Karasek, and Atchley.

kids, but even they were proving to be Rowans. On April 14, Private Russell E. McLogan from Michigan, who had just turned 18, joined Company K, soon showing all the markings of a Rowan. Like most of the kids, he was intelligent, decent, and likeable, but, as happened to so many of these youngsters coming in, the Japs spoiled his chance to capitalize on his mettle. He was soon wounded and spent so much time in the hospital that he didn't get back to the Company until the war was over and the Japanese were no longer thinning our ranks and opening up possibilities for promotion. But he went on in life after the war to become an engineer, a good citizen, and raise a fine family. In retirement he has become a scholar and an historian, writing about about the war and the times.

Guy G. Hinton of West Virginia was a Rowan. He came to my attention when I had the job of censoring soldiers' letters. If there was anything in a letter about our military plans, as if a soldier ever knew of any, or about our present location — which the enemy knew very well since they were seldom farther away than a few hundred yards — we had to

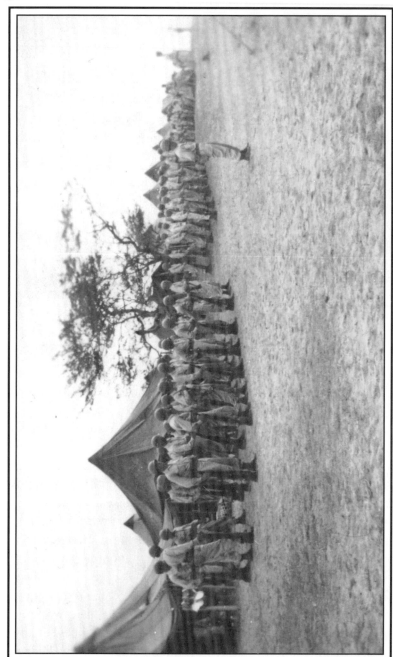

Above and next page: Luzon, September 1945. Peacetime soldiering begins immediately after the surrender: living in tents, military formations.

excise those sentences from their letters. Some of the letters did contain outrageous statements of bragging — fictional accounts of great battles, for example — that weren't the best thing to report. Most amusing were letters that had been cut to shreds to give the impression that writer had been in on some really hot stuff which a censor had to cut out. These we returned. Hinton's letter had none of this baloney. It was simply a beautiful and touching letter to this wife, nothing in it about combat, no complaining; just a letter revealing a fine and gentle man. Whenever I censored, I saw no need to read another of his letters. They belonged only to him and his wife.

Hinton was good looking, but I doubt he knew it. His bearing and quiet manner complemented his looks. His decency and genuineness drew men to him. By instinct he was not a fighter, but he was a superior soldier. He was a gentle man, a family man, a man who would return home to become a credit to his community and raise a fine family. On the day of the cease-fire, a flap of dirt the size of a manhole cover raised up from the ground. A Jap peered out, positioned his rifle, and shot Guy Hinton between the eyes.

Part Three

Sword

Chapter 14

Brave New World

WHEN THE WAR ended, I was still in the hospital. Please, I prayed, if the 6th Division leaves the Philippines for occupation duty in Japan, don't leave me behind. Years before I had been stranded at Fort Dix, when I was in the hospital and my outfit left for England without me. I had lost friends and an outfit; I didn't want to lose them again. Luckily, this time I was returned to Company K now bivouacked along the coast of Luzon facing the China Sea. Weapons and equipment were being cleaned and repaired, clothing was being mended or replaced, gear was being packed, everything was being made ready for loading aboard a ship.

Gone from the men were the drawn faces, the sunken eyes, the jungle rot on their skin, the grubby clothes. The men were scrubbed clean and shaved. The 6th Division was getting ready to occupy a defeated Japan, so we thought. We were at peace. Reprieve. Call us Lazarus. No one can know what it's like to have given up hope of getting through a war alive, then find a new hope in the future. There was, there is, no question in my mind; Truman saved millions of lives, American and Japanese, by dropping the bomb.

Preparations for departure didn't keep us too busy for a swim in the China Sea. Or to sun on the beach with time to read. Or to listen to a radio. We tuned in Shanghai. A commercial came on in English. A restaurant advertised its menu; both Oriental and European dishes were described. If going to the restaurant wasn't possible, just dial 76459, or some such number; the restaurant would deliver the meal to a home. That the restaurant was in business catering to an English-speaking population a month after war's end was impressive, but to dial, that was the surprise. Back home, many Americans still needed an operator to connect them. In the U.S., it was not uncommon to have to ring up the operator by turning a crank.

On short wave, we picked up a reporter somewhere in China talking to his headquarters back in the U.S. In relating a recent trip to Manchuria, he told of the Soviets acting like the United States was an enemy. "Ominous" was a word he kept repeating. After a few minutes of depressing stories of Soviet duplicity, he got down to business, which was to broadcast a report for network radio, the Columbia Broadcasting System, I believe. After a countdown, he spoke on the record to the radio audience, watering down his description of conditions in China and Manchuria. On the record we heard one story, off another.

We, too, were going to have an experience that would open our eyes to the reality of the Soviets. Farewell to the naive notion that peace had been achieved after the fall of Japan. My generation had been ensnared by the folly of the first half of a bloody century, now it looked like the second half would be as grim as the first. We had grown up in a dream world, all too ignorant of the terrible one in which we lived. It cost us dearly. By the '30s, radio had come along with its soap operas, comedy shows, and the Lucky Strike Hit Parade playing the top ten tunes of the week. And there were news broadcasts and Walter Winchell, who machine-gunned his words at us, dramatically giving us the lowdown on the state of the world. But, except for Winchell, our daily life was tranquil. Even after the war, television didn't get into full swing until the mid-'50s to juice up anxieties by bringing the grim pictures of wars and atrocities into our living rooms. Now we have it, and it has destroyed our innocence.

Meanwhile, we awaited a time when we could return home. We were leaving the Philippines, thinking we were headed for Japan.

On October 3, 1945, all the officers of the 3rd Battalion were called to headquarters to learn of plans for embarkation, which would take place on the 10th. Landing craft would be loaded at the beach, then carry us out several miles from shore where we would transfer to a troop ship.

"Munschauer," the Transportation Officer said, pointing to a chart showing the expected ship's various holds and facilities. "You are to be our liaison officer aboard the ship coordinating the loading. Navy has sent instructions for lining up each outfit one after another on shore like this," he said, pointing to another chart showing the battalion's companies strung out in a line one after another to ensure logical placement of men and equipment for transport to the ship. "But we aren't going to put our faith in their plan. It fits the ship the Navy said it is sending, but the Navy has a way of sending a ship different from the one planned. We'll line up like this," he said, pointing to a sketch showing the companies fanned out like spokes from a hub. "This gives us the flexibility to move out in any order for any kind of a ship."

Along with a radio operator who carried a powerful "portable" radio, about the size of a 19-inch TV, strapped to his back, a fast boat took us out to meet the ship before it got to the point of embarkation. Whatever the name of the ship that arrived I cannot remember for sure, but I do remember that it was not the one we expected. Army archives indicate the name was the *Alpine*, I remember it as the *General Gordon*, but I will have to concede to the archivists. With the Marine officer in charge of loading, we went over the *Alpine's* configuration and radioed back information about changes, which were easily made, thanks to Battalion's flexible plan. The 3rd Battalion, along with the rest of the 6th Division, had learned to expect the unexpected and prepare for it. Stories of military inefficiency and bumbling did not apply to the 6th Division, and probably not to any first-rate combat units. For us and for them, it was do or die. Combat units had to be resourceful, to speculate on how conditions might change, to have alternate plans. With the war over, and the fear of death no longer the spur to get things done with the least amount of waste or hassle, the Division undoubtedly drifted into the bureaucratic ways characteristic of big organizations, but for once in my life I had the pleasure of working where muscles were powered by blood that flowed unobstructed through organizational veins that weren't clogged with bureaucratic sludge.

But sometimes military resourcefulness was based more on chicanery than good management. At times it was quicker to replace a smashed jeep by "borrowing" than requisitioning. The Army stole from the Navy and the Navy from the Air Corps, but most of the stealing was of government stuff: a generator, a vehicle, tools, items an outfit needed now and then that would never arrive in time or arrive at all if requisitioned through channels. Sometimes what was stolen was as harmless as ice cream rations, things that for the most part make life better. Stealing, considered more of a game than a crime, was common. It wasn't quite so funny, however, when men stole from each other.

Navy men at sea didn't get much chance to pick up souvenirs, so one way to get them was to snitch them from Army men. That would have been acceptable to us if they stole from the Military Police or quartermaster, but not from infantrymen who are always on the move and seldom get to keep the few souvenirs they find. The few small treasures they might acquire become especially important to them. Some members of the *Alpine* crew had gotten into the hold and had stolen some of our precious stuff. I complained, only to find that my job as liaison officer went beyond helping to load the ship. I should have detailed men to stand guard over our possessions, but that was news to me, received too late to repair the damage. I thought holds were for trucks, weapons, and heavy equipment that I assumed were inaccessible during a voyage.

Land ho! We sailed by small rocky islands no bigger than football fields. Small pagodas or shrines on some of them added charm. Japan was going to be interesting, exciting. But if this was a part of Japan, we weren't going to see it. We sailed right past the islands and into the Yellow Sea heading for Korea, slowed along the way by a typhoon.

Plowing into it, the ship would ride up and up on a wave, giving the feeling of rising on a fast-moving elevator, then having made its way over the crest, down, down, down went the elevator until the ship shoved its nose into the trough of the next wave. There, the bow scooped up half the ocean and tossed it back over itself.

Bad as it is to head into waves, taking them broadside is worse. On the USS *Golden City* heading for home in December, I learned what broadsides were like during a violent storm off the coast of Alaska. With each hit of a wave we rolled so far over that the sewer outlets dipped below the ship's water line, backing up toilet drains and shooting geysers of sewage under unfortunate "sitters." The trick was to to jump on a toilet just after she had spouted, do your business fast, and get off before the ship rolled back to produce another geyser. And getting anywhere in the ship was, in itself, a challenge as you were slammed from one side of the passage to the other with each roll.

Fortunately, I survived the ships as well as the war.

Chapter 15

Muck

HE 1993 EDITION of the *Columbia Encyclopedia* lists the 1985 population of Inchon, Korea, as 1,386,000. It's described as a major industrial city and Korea's second largest port. Impossible. That couldn't be the same woebegone place as the Inchon I stared at from the deck of the *Alpine* waiting to climb down its side on a net into a landing craft. A major industrial city? From the ship, anchored a distance offshore, there wasn't any sign of the kind of multi-storied structures typical of a metropolis. What we could see were the usual harbor trappings, cranes for handling, low warehouse buildings, and smaller buildings beyond, houses perhaps, looking like they were made of mud. Many miracles happened in the years after the war, and Korea's emergence from a rustic colony of Japan to a sophis-

ticated country is one of them. Inchon must have been at the forefront of
this transformation.

But a major port? Even today that is hard to believe. Inchon is on the
Yellow Sea at a place where the tides are enormous, making navigation
difficult. We were anchored a good half-mile out to sea, otherwise our
ship would have lain on a mud flat when the tide went out. While we
were waiting for the tide to be at full flood to travel to shore in landing
crafts, Korean vessels, round-bottom affairs the size of large Chinese
junks, lay on their bottoms in endless muck, waiting for the flood tide to
float them.

Some time later, while bivouacked along the coast south of Inchon, I
was issued a new rifle. Its sights had to be zeroed in — adjusted. The
way to do it is to shoot at a target. If the bullet lands to the left of the target, for example, to compensate the sight has to be adjusted for the next
shot to land more to the right. To get it perfect might take four or five
shots. I tried to rig a target, but everywhere I turned somebody was
working the land, weeding, harvesting, planting, or carrying water. Or
urinating! Better to set up at a target offshore. When the tide was out, I
shot into the muck, figuring that when the first shot landed, a splatter of
mud would mark a target. Never expecting anyone to be out in the muck,
I was startled when a clamdigger sprung up like a bee had stung him as
the bullet landed near him. I fired my rifle farther out and in a different
direction. This time five clamdiggers rose up, all screaming and waving
to warn me off. Then five times five and five times that again rose up to
take up the warning. In short order, as far as I could see, the mud flats
were alive with clamdiggers.

This was the kind of tidal area we had to cross to get to shore at
Inchon. Anything to screw up the timing would have left landing craft
mired in the muck. MacArthur had to contend with the same situation
when he made his end run around the North Koreans to land at Inchon
during the Korean War. Common sense should have told him that the
chance for screw-ups was so great that the venture was foolhardy. But he
was lucky, and thus his maneuver was considered brilliant. A small
amount of enemy fire could have slowed his operation and left hundreds
of landing craft stuck in the mud, to be picked off like sitting ducks. My
salute goes to the Navy for bringing it off.

Inchon's harbor did have a tidal basin with gates to let ships in and out of the harbor at flood and to hold water in and the ships afloat when the tide was out. For a large commercial harbor, however, the ships using the basin didn't look nearly as large as the *Alpine,* which was only about 13,000 gross tons. Perhaps later the basin was enlarged to help make Inchon a major port.

Our diversion from Japan to Korea smacked of a last-minute decision. We received no briefing, no orientation to tell us about the Koreans and their country, no information about their relationship with Japan to give us an historical perspective. All we were told was that Korea was occupied by Japanese troops who had been ordered by their emperor to surrender to us. Japanese troops? Occupied? I thought Korea had been integrated into Japan so long ago that it was essentially Japanese. We knew as little about Korea as the Koreans knew about us.

As we went ashore, Du Kim, or whatever his name was, peered out at us from behind a fence. He wasn't old, but he looked it, wearing a tall top hat like Abraham Lincoln's, except that below the brim was something like a skull cap that helped to secure the hat to his head. Instead of calling him Du Kim I might have called him Dr. Fu Manchu because, like the good doctor, wispy hairs hung from his chin in an anemic goatee. His shirt was white, as were his loose-hanging knickers. He might have been a carpenter or a shoemaker. Perhaps a tradesman. I could never find out. I spoke to many Du Kims but never found one that could speak English. Or if they could, they wouldn't.

More important than to know his trade would have been to know what made him tick, what he thought. His country had been dominated from 1392 to 1910 by the repressive Confucian Yi dynasty, then after that by Japanese who fed a line that suited their purpose. We didn't have to speak the language to know that they never heard anything good about us. And they seemed to have believed what they heard. Americans may have been waved into Paris and even Rome in a great celebration of liberation, but no one in Korea treated us as liberators.

If Du Kim lived to be a hundred he would always remember the wave after wave of landing craft that dumped us on his shores. Japan was supposed to have power, but they had nothing like this. Whoever we were, he had been badly misled, but we didn't mistreat him. Eventually, because we stayed around so long, he might have become accustomed to the way we looked, though at the time he thought we were ugly. He might have been one of many Korean communists who had their own plans for revolt against Japan, and now we were coming to steal his revolution. He would have been glad if we were Russians, because they had supported him. He hated us because we were to move his country in the opposite direction from where he thought it ought to go. And our customs were to clash with his, making him think we were weird. But before any of this could happen, we had to settle in.

After landing on October 18, we spent the night on the concrete floor of a warehouse in the rail yards that served the harbor. Never did I think I would ever again want to carve a hole in the ground to sleep in, but that night I would have welcomed the chance. The floor was freezing; the ground was warm. The ground could be shaped to my body; the floor was unyielding.

The second night we moved to a textile factory and were issued Army cots, the kind with canvas stretched on a wood frame. At least we could sleep off the floor, but, with the night, rats arrived. No sooner would I fall asleep than I'd be awakened by the scurrying creatures. My pack was a favorite target. I spent the night flailing my rifle at them to chase them off. The concrete floor back in the rail yard didn't look so bad after all.

In battle, soldiers go on for weeks living in clothes soaked from the inside with sweat and from the outside with slop and mud. But let the battle subside and they will find water somewhere to get clean. They will find a peasant woman to beat their clothes with a stick over a rock in a stream to drive out dirt the Philippine way. They will find other comforts. If they are huddled in foxholes surviving on K rations and there are chickens at a nearby farm, you can be sure they will soon be eating chicken. If there is a watermelon patch nearby, they will find it and enjoy watermelon. Not far from where we were staying, these sorts of good things were available.

Near our location the second night in Korea, there was a small inn run by a Japanese family. The next night, seven of us stayed in the inn and had our first lesson in Japanese culture. Upon entering, in response to the innkeeper's amusing attempt at mime, which made us laugh but got his message across, we took off our boots and put on slippers. Bowing and smiling and laughing along with us, he led us into an unfurnished room, except for a ceramic urn in the center as big as a large pumpkin. Inside the urn glowed a disk of compressed charcoal, warming the room

— most welcome for us, coming as we did from the tropics to a cold climate. Again with mime and by gently pushing us to where he wanted us to be, we were soon sitting on a floor of woven mats arranged around the urn. Although the room was plain, it was pleasant. Sliding translucent panels defined the perimeter. Then, like spring flowers coming up through snow, Cio-cio-san entered, changing the entire aspect.

A room's harmony is usually created by decor and architectural detail, but here these features were understated to highlight the presence of this beautiful woman and her exquisite kimono. Cio-cio-san appeared to be about 15, yet she moved with the grace and charm of an experienced dancer. She was carrying a tea service from which she served us with ceremony. An occasional giggle of embarrassment reminded us that she was still a child. We were enthralled. All that was missing was Puccini's music.

In our heavy olive-drab uniforms we felt out of place, all the more so because we were dirty. And we were tired — dead tired after two nights with little sleep and not much before that on board ship, where we were kept on the alert, dressed, and waiting for orders to disembark. Drooping eyelids and nodding heads made it unnecessary for us to resort to mime to let the innkeeper know what we needed. Panels were slid back opening the way to another part of the inn. Bedding was placed on the floor in a room large enough for all of us.

With mime of a more embarrassing nature, I indicated my need to go to the bathroom. As I squatted over a long slit trench constructed of tile instead of dirt, my chin stuck forward to give me balance, positioning me to look toward what seemed to be a steam room. I saw a tub shaped like a half a whiskey barrel, only many times larger and with staves of highly polished pine instead of slivery oak. Four smaller buckets about the size of a pail were on the floor. The floor itself was ceramic with drains. This was for me. Tired as I was, sleep could wait.

Stripping, I dipped the pail into the large tub, scooped up a gallon or so of water, and dumped it over myself. Just then, Cio-cio-san entered, let out a yelp, and ran, undoubtedly embarrassed to see an ugly naked man with a very red face and — from wearing a uniform that covered me from the burning tropical sun — a very white body. The contrast between my dark face and white body must have been startling.

But she was back in a flash, this time with the innkeeper, who began chattering at me in a way that told me he was scolding. With that, the two of them took hold of me. The next thing I knew I was in the tub, and they began scrubbing me with a brush. Never before or since have I been pushed around so pleasurably.

At last, to bed, ready to place myself under the spell of the god of sleep and a retinue of dreams, but it was to be Cio-cio-san, not Morpheus, who entranced me. Tiptoeing in, she jumped between my covers and began giggling and squirming. From the giggling and laughing in other parts of the room, I could tell I wasn't the only one with a butterfly in his bed. But with that, an agitated old woman came in and chased the girls away. Just as I was falling back asleep, I sensed that not all the girls had left the room; to my amazement, I discovered the old woman was doing the bed snuggling.

> Last night I crept
> To where she slept
> When supper was done
> And had some fun
>> From *Japanese Inn* by Oliver Statler. ©
>> 1961 by Oliver Statler. Reprinted by per-
>> mission of Random House, Inc.

A captain I met in Luzon who had been a prisoner of war told me the Japanese were intrigued by how much bigger Americans were than they. "And we were hardly captured when they made us drop our pants to check the size of our genitals." Perhaps the same curiosity motivated the old woman. Poor thing. My battery was dead. With so little sleep, Morpheus was the only one with power over us.

Our next stop was to be Kunsan down the coast, the future home of our battalion headquarters. The trip was to be made on a Korean train. I expected something primitive, just a box with four wheels, probably unheated. Not so. Korea had an amazing railroad system. Some towns that looked like they were populated by no more than a few thousand people had railroad yards large enough to serve a metropolis. Most surprising were the railroad cars. Coaches were as good as any on the Lehigh Valley Railroad back home. True, they needed maintenance, but here as well as in the U.S., resources and manpower concentrated on war production, not sprucing up passenger trains. But essentials like heating the cars were kept up. A good thing. The weather had turned bitterly cold.

❧

We awaited our train at a station in the outskirts of Seoul. Trains came and went. Locomotives discharged steam that lingered in the cold air with our breath. The air was invigorating. Soldiers laughed and joked and enjoyed a bit of horseplay. Atchley grabbed Johnson's hat and tossed it to Bryant. Bryant tossed it to Barent. Johnson, happily playing the game, tried to grab it back. Koreans watched, showing neither approval nor disapproval. Would these people never smile or scowl — do something other than just stare at us? The Japanese at the inn, who had reason to hate us, smiled and laughed and seemed to be genuinely friendly. That may have been a front. We met a Japanese lady, an intelligent woman who spoke English, who inquired about where we had fought. When we told her Luzon, she said she had a son in a medical unit there. I thought of the night the Japanese medics fell into our trap and had been slaughtered. Before I could stop him, a soldier told her about the encounter, laughingly adding that if her son was on Luzon he was probably killed. She forced herself to laugh along with him.

Our train, we were told, would be held up to give priority to another coming in from North Korea. Never will I forget seeing it come down the track. People were perched on the cow catcher, people were hanging from the sides of freight cars, people were sitting on the edge of open widows of jammed passenger cars. Windowless boxcars were packed with people. People rode on the roofs. Those with a decent perch clung to small bundles, probably their only possessions. Those without a perch probably dropped their worldly wealth along the way. Some had nothing more to lose; they had frozen to death. What terrible things were happening in North Korea for these people to risk their lives on this train to escape to the south? It had to have involved the Russians who were occupying the north. I remembered the reporter — the American, in China — we had heard back in the Philippines who was broadcasting from Shanghai.

About 12 people got off the train. An engineer, black with soot, jumped from the engine with an oil can in one hand and a wrench in the other, tightened a few connections, and oiled the bearings that tied the connecting rods to the pistons and wheels. That finished, the engine let off a blast of steam and the train moved on. A few passengers that had gotten off arranged their bundles and left. Others just stood around awhile, looking about the way people do when they are expecting someone. No one came. Finally, only a couple remained, the woman clinging to a bundle in her arms and the man who had been riding on the top of a boxcar. The few railroad workers ignored them. Our soldiers, who had been watching with disbelief all that had happened, began to sense that something must be terribly wrong, otherwise the couple wouldn't just stand there for so long like they were cast in stone. Curiosity got the better of a soldier who approached the pair — at first just to have a look, then to try to ask if he could help.

What did these bewildered Koreans think? At first one soldier came over to stare at them; then they were surrounded by many. These soldiers had eyes and skin and faces just like Russians. They were trying to talk to them in a language as strange as that of the Russians in the north from whom they had fled. Could they tell from the tone of voice that these soldiers were trying to be friendly and compassionate? What they sensed they did not show. A soldier moved closer, first touching the precious bundle, then gently pulling down the blanket that was wrapped around it. The woman did not pull back. Nor did she resist when he gently took the bundle from her. Good God, it was a baby. A dead baby. Tears rolled down the soldier's cheek. But the couple did not cry. If they had cried, they did it some time ago. The baby had been dead a day or more.

The soldier took the baby and carried it to a grassy place beside the station where others removed their trench shovels from their packs and dug a grave. With bowed heads and in prayer they buried the child while the couple watched. We, strangers from a far-off place, did this strange thing. Could these simple people sense that the soldiers wished to be kind? Or did they think us barbarous?

The funeral was not enough. Compassion demanded more. A soldier took off his helmet, put some money in it, and passed it around. Fistfuls of yen, more money than the couple might have ever seen in a lifetime, was jammed into that helmet and held out to the couple. When they made no attempt to accept it, the money was stuffed into their pockets. Our train came in. No one said anything. We just turned and climbed aboard. As we pulled away, I looked back. The couple was walking slowly toward the town. In less than a minute the engine had the train up to full speed, and soldiers, still not speaking, stared out the windows.

We passed a play yard. Kids could be seen running around, laughing and yelling. Our noses were pressed against the train's windows, as we watched in amazement. Similar to a teeter-totter, a plank was placed over a fulcrum in the fashion of a seesaw. But instead of sitting at the ends of the board seesaw fashion, the kids stood on the ends, the one on the rising end taking advantage of his momentum to fly into the air when he reached the top; that thrill over, he came down to land on the board with as much force as possible to send the other end of the teeter-totter up and his partner flying. The idea seemed to be how high they could toss each other. What fun. And what skill for kids so small; some couldn't have been much more than five. As we started to talk about the games and the crazy things we did as kids, the incident back at the station was forgotten. Battle veterans don't keep sad memories. They can't afford them.

Chapter 16

Haystacks and Chest Hair

AT KUNSAN, the three rifle companies of the Battalion were each sent to different areas of southwestern Korea. K Company headed inland from the Yellow Sea coast in a motor convoy, troops armed and riding in trucks — Company Commander leading in a command car, top down, machine-gun mounted, ready for trouble. We were headed to where Japanese troops were still armed — 3,751 of them. No trouble was expected, but there could be dissident elements unwilling to accept the surrender. Better to be prepared.

Half an afternoon out from Kunsan along a country road, the convoy came to a sudden halt. Ahead a quarter-mile or so a haystack stood in the middle of the road, blocking it. If it was some kind of a bunker concealing a cannon, they could easily blast us. Nothing happened. We moved ahead slowly. The haystack began to move. We stopped again. Whoever was in command of the haystack was about to reveal his intentions. Hesitatingly, the haystack moved to the side of the road, making way for us to pass. Accepting this as a friendly gesture, we moved ahead. As we pulled alongside, we saw feet beneath the stack. In the middle of it, partially hidden by the hay, we could make out a peasant's shoulder and head. Farther into the countryside we encountered more and more haystacks making their way down the road.

Our troubles were not over. As we neared a village, someone was standing in the middle of the road with what appeared to be a gun. Field glasses showed it to be a rifle. No one else seemed to be with the rifle-man, save peasants working in the field. Several officers in the lead ve-hicles surveyed the area with field glasses. All they saw were more farm-ers. We moved ahead slowly, every soldier tense and on the alert. Who-ever was ahead stepped to the side of the road to let us pass. As we came alongside, a young lad with a toy rifle waved to us.

We hadn't gone unnoticed in the village. As we drew closer we could see a crowd gathering. When we entered, the crowd pulled back. We dis-mounted to stretch and give our fannies a rest from the truck's hard benches. The villagers scrambled, running for the safety of their shops and homes, leaving the center of the town empty. Finally a door opened. A child peeked out. Before his mother could pull him back, he got away from her and ran toward us. When none of us tried to eat him, another door opened; this time an old man appeared. We smiled. He smiled. He walked over to look at a jeep. Nothing terrible happened to him. More doors began to open. Soon we were surrounded by villagers laughing and talking and pointing to our faces. My shirt was opened. My chest is not hairy, but a few hairs showed. A villager kept staring at them, final-ly grabbing them with a yank. I learned much later that the Koreans were fascinated by our chest hair and referred to us as monkeys. We were strange men, white, hairy, with strange eyes, altogether ugly-looking. We and they were laughing together, but they were having the better time, the kind of fun people have looking at animals in a zoo. At last I saw Koreans laughing and talking.

Several villages and an hour later, a major who had been riding in a jeep moved ahead of the command car and signaled for the column to halt. He pulled my platoon and led us to a town hall where we were told to get our gear and set up headquarters. I was to find a Japanese regiment occupying the town and disarm them. He didn't know whether any prior arrangements had been made for them to meet me. All the major could give me was a sketch showing where to find what turned out to be 1,592 men of the 464th Japanese Regiment. I had not known the number of soldiers or the name of the regiment in advance of my search.

The major left me without a map, which might show the location of this town in relation to the rest of Korea; nor did I have any information about the town, its size, or its industry — nothing except its name, Kumje. I was in charge. But to do what, except disarm soldiers? We were left a jeep and a promise that the major would be back sometime soon with more instructions.

With Sergeant Johnson staying behind at the town hall where we decided to get settled, and the day already showing dusk, I set out to find the Japanese commander. I sensed hundreds of eyes following me as I made my way through the streets of Kumje. I saw no one. Rounding a corner, I found a marker that, according to the sketch, was the street that led to the Japanese headquarters, except that it was no street, just a narrow alley, and a dark one as the afternoon was late. A Japanese soldier peered out from a gate in a fence, saw me, froze, then turned and ran, which was what I wanted to do. I wished I had brought a gun, although I knew it was wise not to.

At the end of the alley I found a barracks. A Japanese officer, obviously aware that I was coming, saluted when I came into sight. Much to my surprise he greeted me in good English. I had been dreading this meeting, imagining all sorts of things, including getting shot or at least a sullen reception. I had gone without a weapon because I didn't think even the Japanese would take advantage of an unarmed man. What I found was an officer perfectly reconciled to the defeat of his country and deeply concerned about the welfare of his troops and the Japanese civilians in town. They lived in fear of certain Korean elements who promised to avenge the Japanese occupation. For their protection, he had been occupying the town militarily, posting his soldiers at various key points; but he was ready to call in his men and give up his weapons.

What I didn't need was a town gone wild ransacking and pillaging Japanese homes, possibly killing soldiers and civilians. Much, I think, to

Lieutenant Karasek and Sergeant Johnson at a Japanese ammunition shelter, Kunsan Airdrome, Korea, November 1945.

Lieutenant Munschauer and Sergeant Johnson standing in front of a Japanese barracks at the Kunsan Airdrome, Korea, November 1945.

Sergeant Johnson
standing on a
Japanese monument,
November 1945, at
the Japanese Kunsan
Airdrome, Korea.

the astonishment of the Japanese commander, and I am sure to the em-
bitterment of some Koreans, I decided that because it was late, the
Japanese soldiers could keep their weapons and man their posts until the
next morning, at which point we would be better prepared to take over
the town. In the morning we replaced the Japanese at their posts, let
them store their weapons, and, following their routines, continued the
mission of protecting homes and persons. I don't know if anything
would have happened if we had not done so. I suspect that some things
did go on behind the scenes, possibly revenge taken against Korean collaborators. My suspicion was heightened when sometime later I went to

Lieutenant Munschauer beside a Japanese barracks, November 1945, at the Japanese Kunsan Airdrome, Korea.

find a Korean pharmacist who supposedly spoke English, but never found him. He had disappeared. However, the town, on the surface, remained calm, leaving us without much to do except carry on routine patrols to show our presence.

The surrounding terrain was flat, but as I got farther into the country-side I found areas that reminded me of my own section of New York state with its rolling hills, wooded areas, fruit trees, and some open lands planted in wheat or hay. The Korean grain fields were ripe for harvest, almost past because we were well into the fall. I went to see the grain being harvested. What I saw stopped me in my tracks. Korean thugs with guns had the farmers lined up in a row, military-style, forcing the harvesters, as they worked their way across the field, to swing their scythes in the rhythm of slaves at the oars of a long boat.

Because the mayor and other Korean officials who had been in place under Japanese occupation hadn't been removed, I thought that the town was carrying on as usual. But these officials had been mere puppets; the Japanese had wielded the actual power. Unknown to me, a self-appointed group had taken over the town and the surrounding community. Now that the Japanese were out of they way, the goons were pulling the strings, so I conjectured. Keeping the Korean puppets in their jobs created an illusion of a stable government. I wondered what happened to the puppets after we left.

With the Japanese officer as an interpreter — embarrassing, but there were no Koreans who spoke English — I sought the leader of the agricultural workers. His entire government showed up at my headquarters: the minister of justice, the chief of security, the agricultural director, the minister of culture, the economics advisor, and more — all with pretentious titles, all big bruisers; and all, while they said little, conveyed a feeling of contempt toward me. As long as I was in town, I said, things were not going to be done by bullying. I fumbled with some thoughts about democracy, but nothing could have been more futile, especially with the words coming to them via a Japanese interpreter. Several days later the major showed up in his jeep. What the hell was going on? We were late into the fall, there was an impending food shortage, and the grain wasn't being harvested. Much to my relief — because I didn't see how I could go to the goons and eat crow — somehow the farmers worked things out and the grain did get harvested.

If my relations with the Koreans were problematic, those with the Japanese were cordial. Perhaps they shouldn't have been. They were the oppressors. If we were interested in ingratiating ourselves with anyone, it should have been with the oppressed. Korea was the country to rebuild, the country whose friendship and respect we should cultivate, the country to have as an ally in the northeastern continent of Asia, where Russia and China dominated. But I knew nothing of global politics. I couldn't befriend the Koreans; they couldn't befriend me — at least not easily, given the language barrier. Several of the Japanese families were highly educated, well travelled, and spoke English. And when

I was invited to the home of the leading Japanese citizen, I readily accepted.

My grandmother had a large home furnished with heavy carved-oak furniture, the living room featuring a huge table in the middle, the couches and upholstered chairs backed up against the walls, smaller chairs in position ready to be pulled up to the big table. This was where the family gathered. There was another room, more formal, the furniture spindly and white with velvety red upholstery. A marble bust was perched on a tall stand. A big mirror with a white frame reflected its formality. We kids were told not to go in that room, and above all not to sit on the furniture, which we had no desire to do anyway — it looked horribly uncomfortable. I asked my mother what the room was for. "For guests," she said. "It's where your grandmother receives callers. It's called a parlor."

In the Japanese home I was received in the equivalent of my grandmother's parlor — not one furnished like hers, although the furniture was as uncomfortable, being an imitation of Western-style upholstered easy chairs with the legs cut short. We sat with our knees above our belly buttons. A picture of a suffering Christ dominated the room, like my grandmother's mirror. We had a cup of tea and chatted about this and that. By way of small talk, my host mentioned he had visited Niagara Falls. Here was something to talk about. I lived near the Falls, saw it often, and was forever fascinated by it. We found something in common. Rapport was established. Suddenly he asked if he might excuse himself. When he left I went over to the picture of Christ and moved it to the side a bit to see if the wall might be of a different color. I wondered if the picture had been hanging for a long time, or if it had been quickly put up for my benefit. It *had* been hanging for sometime.

My host returned with a collection of small silver souvenir spoons collected while traveling in America. Selecting one saying "Niagara Falls," he insisted I have it. Then we stepped outside to inspect his gardens. With pride he took me to a courtyard featuring sand raked in various designs and filled with rocks. I recall being in Dublin once to see the Book of Kells. A gauche tourist looking down at this marvelously illuminated manuscript remarked, "You mean we waited in line all this time to see this?" As my Japanese host waxed enthusiastically over his sandpile, I am afraid I listened with a bored look, showing myself to be as boorish as the tourist in not appreciating an important form of art. I now deeply regret not taking the opportunity to ask my host more about the meaning of the garden, and of the other art in his home.

When we learned we would have to leave Korea and could take only what we could carry, we showed ourselves to be fair in purchasing some Japanese goods, mostly kimonos. The Japanese, too, would be limited in what they could take home. We could have acted like conquistadors, taking their jewelry and art, which not only had personal meaning for them but was also the one source of wealth they could take back to Japan. And without our presence, the Koreans could easily have looted their homes, although I saw no indication that such a thing would happen. The Japanese got off easy, which is not the way things were when they were the conquerors.

Yet we did not go unappreciated. A bowing Japanese gentleman appeared at my headquarters one afternoon with an invitation for me and two of my "adjutants" to attend a banquet to be given in my honor. Considering our relations with the Koreans, it might have been wiser politically to decline, but how could I resist? As directed, with my two "adjutants," Sergeants Johnson and Timmerman, I arrived at the appointed hour, in the same Japanese home where I had been before. This time we were escorted beyond the room with the sawed-off furniture and the portrait of Jesus to a large dining room where everything was in the style of Japan.

The other guests, 25 or so, all of them men, were already positioned on the floor — I can't say seated — around a U-shaped table, sitting with their legs tucked under them, their feet somehow turned out so that they could sit on them more comfortably. Try as we could, neither my adjutants nor I could figure out how to tuck our legs under Japanese-style — we couldn't even figure out how they could tuck their feet under their haunches! It seemed anatomically impossible. We had to sit on the floor with our legs forward, sticking them under the table, which meant that in this shoe-less Japanese home our stocking feet stuck out the other side. Happily, our socks didn't have holes. But even to us Americans there was something inelegant about this, like being at a banquet at the Ritz in an undershirt. At least, because we all sat on the outside of the U, no one sat across from us where they would have to contend with our feet in their face.

Right away I could see we were in for a drinking contest. A beautiful young girl snuggled next to me with a decanter ever ready to fill my cup with sake. My host explained quite proudly that she was a very special geisha who had been brought in from a distant city just for this occasion. She would be performing special dances. And from the way she kept filling my cup and trying to get me to drink, I had a feeling she would get a bonus if she got me drunk. Furthermore, my host whispered to me — he could no longer keep the big secret — she was to be mine for the night. At the end of the evening she would go home with me.

Drinks were being pressed on my sergeants as well, and I couldn't help worrying about this drinking contest after my experience in Guagua. I got a good warning from my own spinning head that told me to watch the drinks — a difficult task with a geisha on my left and my host on the right. I couldn't tell you what we ate, but I did take in the way the food was served. The party was an all-male affair, but the men's wives, dressed for the occasion in gorgeous kimonos and moving with grace and ceremony, served the food. I could see enough of the entrance to the kitchen to note that these Japanese women didn't have to sweat over a hot stove or dirty their hands in a dishpan. Peasant women brought the dishes as far as the dining room door where the wives took over.

By chance I looked out the dining room windows which were large, somewhat like modern sliding-glass doors. Despite the darkness, I caught a glimpse of several Japanese soldiers peering in. Automatically I wanted to reach for a gun. My stomach cramped. If you can imagine looking down to see a python crawling up your pant leg, then you can imagine how the sight of Japanese soldiers hit me. But I calmed down and realized that the banquet was a big event and the soldiers, now unarmed and free to roam, had decided to peek in on the fun.

The meal progressed with much formality in the serving. The geisha danced and sang in the space in the middle of the table. During the performances the wives came into the dining room and stood in the background to watch. Next came the grand event. My host told me that a leading Japanese citizen would be making a speech. He came over to the other side of the table in front of me and bowed very low. I returned the bow. It seemed like the thing to do. Then he knelt before me and bowed to the floor. I bowed again. Speaking Japanese, he began in a normal voice that, as he got into the spirit of his oration, grew louder and louder, rising and falling, sounding like someone singing a Gregorian chant on a roller coaster, punctuated now and then with a chicken squawk, all the time bowing before my feet as if they were an idol being prayed to. Finally, obviously quite satisfied with himself, he stood and bowed to me and the others. I asked my host what he said.

"He wanted you to know he appreciated the treatment they were receiving."

"Is that all?"

"Oh, there was much more, but it all said the same thing."

When it was well past midnight and time to go, we were drunk, but, thank God, well behaved. With fond farewells like we had been buddies all our lives, and with truly good feelings all around, we three left, arm in arm — with the geisha.

Then it hit me: we were drunk, barely able to walk a straight line, and only able to do so with the support of the geisha, and we would be arriving at the barracks with a woman in tow. We had no private quarters, all of us sleeping cot beside cot in a big room. What would the men think? And in my condition, would I have any control over the platoon if things got out of hand? I never thought the girl would be coming with us. And if I had had my wits about me, I would have said thank you, but no thank you. But here she was. Or was she? She had guided us down the dark streets and back alleys of the deserted Kumje, and when we turned the corner to our street, she was gone.

Apparently the Koreans were aware that I had been entertained by the Japanese, and they were not to be outdone. They, too, invited me to a banquet. We gathered at a restaurant at midday. Thank God were was no sake and no long speeches, just a luncheon. But there was a nice feeling about the affair, sort of like a Rotary Club meeting, lots of smiles, good conversation I guessed, although I didn't understand a word. Old friends, again just men, greeted each other. The affair was obviously a special occasion.

We had a clear soup with some things floating in it, vegetables, a pasta, and the *pièce de résistance*, a large eyeball. The Koreans with some show, like men about to sip a vintage wine, raised the eyeball on their chopsticks and popped it into their mouths with gusto. I tried, but just as I would get it close to my mouth it slid off the sticks and plopped back into my soup. At the far end of the table I noticed several of the men whispering. One of them rose and left out a back door, reappearing shortly with a spoon, probably borrowed from a Japanese. Now, with all eyes on me, I scooped up the eyeball and, pretending to show enjoyment, I swallowed it. Nothing to it — slid down just like an oyster.

The next day several of the Rotary types from the luncheon, all smiling with much joviality, dropped by my quarters with a Japanese as interpreter. Would I like to go for a drive to see the countryside? We would have to use my jeep as none of them had a car, so they said. A date was set for the next week for what proved to be a beautiful fall day. I looked forward to the outing. With my driver and me in front and three of them squeezed in back, and without the interpreter, we took off. At the first village a delegation awaited us. A small platform had been erected; a crowd had gathered. My hosts shook hands with the local big-wigs. I was introduced. The speeches began. They were short, and while I didn't understand a word, I could tell from the way the Koreans were punctuating their words by smiling and turning to me, that they were implying that I stood four-square behind them.

I had been set up. I felt like a patsy. I was participating in a political rally, for what cause I did not know. At least I didn't see any of the goons who had brutalized the farmers at harvest. We went from village to village, political rally to political rally, and I was stuck because I didn't know how to turn back without the Koreans pointing the way.

⚓

While I was being marshalled around the countryside as an unwilling actor in a charade for what purpose I knew not, a delegation of Japanese soldiers and officers, all very formal, all spit and polish, came to my quarters to express their appreciation for the way I had treated them — dignity seemed to be the word they were trying to use. Because I wasn't there, and because they were about to leave Kumje and could not return, Sergeant Johnson acted on my behalf for what turned out to be a ceremony. On my return, excited soldiers couldn't wait to tell me about it. "Boy, oh boy, Lieutenant, did you ever miss a great show!" The Japanese captain had made a speech, there was much saluting and bowing, and, for the grand finale, they left their regimental sergeant major's sword for me, a weapon I still proudly display. I remain forever sorry I missed that event, but at least I have the sword.

Soon after, the Japanese civilians also left Kumje. They departed not as "Japs," which is how I saw them at first, but as Japanese. From seeing them as barbarians, as people of whom the very sight made me sick, I began to see them as a civilization with a culture to admire. My original distaste for them gave way to acceptance and finally to friendship. I had, after all, previously learned to admire and like their ilk back in the United States when I was at Fort McClellan training Nisei, a generation born in the United States of immigrant Japanese. And although they were not really Japanese — they were Americans — their admirable qualities came from their Japanese parents.

I have read *The Harp of Burma*, a Japanese novel about an infantry company; and I have read *The Naked and the Dead*, Norman Mailer's story of American Infantrymen on patrol who surprised a group of Japanese soldiers in a situation very similar to our experience on patrol in the Philippines. I did not know Mailer's soldiers. They were a nasty bunch. I knew the soldiers in the Japanese story. They killed to be sure because they had to; but they cared for each other, they were scared, and they loved life for the things in life that are worthwhile. They were like the Americans with whom I served.

Yet, when I think about the Japanese as a people, I waver in my feeling for them. Not all the soldiers in *The Harp of Burma* were admirable. Some, in a display of fanaticism, stupidly and stubbornly refused to surrender at the end of the war. The author did not take us into the minds of these fanatics to show us what made them tick. If he had, we might have understood; but perhaps he himself had no use for them. He only revealed the heart and the soul of his principal heroes, courageous men with a sense of honor. The author did, however, inadvertently reveal something about the Japanese that is disturbing.

In the book, his heroes were imprisoned by the British at the end of the war and put to work preparing a cemetery for hundreds and hundreds of British soldiers who died of cholera and abuse while prisoners of the Japanese. The author portrays his soldiers as going about their task with great respect for the British as honorable men who happened to be victims of war. The novel doesn't even hint that the British died from the cruelty of and neglect by their captors, not from the fortunes of war. The Japanese committed atrocities. They should face up to them. But they won't. The author of *The Harp of Burma* wouldn't. And thus, like an individual who will deny what he has done and won't face up to his mistakes, these are a people difficult to trust.

Chapter 17

This Is Where
I Came In

THE DEPARTURE of the Japanese around early November left no reason for us to remain in Kumje. We rejoined the rest of Company K, stationed at a former Japanese airfield near the coast just south of Kunsan. There we had even less to do. Sake was as available.

Dick Fleming, our Company Commander, had long gone back to the States and was replaced by a young West Point graduate who had come over from Europe, having served in combat there. As a Regular Army man, he knew what to do with us.

Hours on end were devoted to close order drill, "Right face, left face, forward march, to the rear, to the rear," etc. It was just like the old Army before the war began. I felt like I had witnessed a great drama and now it was over. It was time to leave; this was where I came in. Because I had been a medical officer who had never had to contend with weapons, I kept forgetting to yell, "Right shoulder arms," and the other commands that had to do with weapons. As a result, when I gave a command to march, the soldiers' weapons might still be resting on the ground, creating minor chaos — not the way to please the West Pointer who wanted to make points toward a promotion by having a sharp, well-drilled company.

Worse, a tragedy was about to make his stay something of a disaster. Men were billeted in a former Japanese barracks — great, long, single-story structures, four men to a room, each room lined up on either side of a long corridor the length of a football field. The weather had turned bitterly cold but the rooms had potbellied stoves, excellent for warmth and for heating sake — which is the best way to drink it.

We officers had smaller quarters, more like cabins. And like the men in the barracks, we, too, had potbellied stoves, which we enjoyed for the same reasons. We might get a visit from one or two of the men, usually after they had had a bit of sake and felt like talking to a father figure — which I had become at the ripe old age of 26. If I had taken that role seriously, we would have listened to them like fathers, but some of them were men I had been with on Hell's Hill and elsewhere, and soon we would be talking like a couple of buddies in a bar who were slightly oiled.

It seemed like it was time to get rid of us wartime officers. We blended too well with the enlisted ranks. In battle an Infantry officer, at least at the platoon level, fights beside his men and sleeps in a hole next to them. He can't remain aloof from them and be a successful leader. Dick Fleming, K Company commander, sized up each new private coming into his company as a potential poker player and a drinking buddy. But he could put all that aside when in a battle and the men would follow him. A great officer had to be bold and smart; he had to respect, even love, his men. If he did, the men would know it and would follow him.

But in peacetime Korea, there was no opportunity to be bold and smart and to show the kind of love that exists between men who will die for each other. Rank had to be used as a source of power and to maintain rank meant keeping some distance between officers and men. I doubt Dick could have done that. In peacetime we needed a standoffish strict guy like the new West Pointer, a guy who would demand discipline. In battle, given good leadership and a war to believe in, everyone pulls together, after the shirkers and the cowards are weeded out in the first skirmishes. In peacetime, the enlisted men's agenda often diverges from their officers', but it is the officers' agenda that must be followed. The West Pointer had the rank, the bearing, and the will to get his way. He was gradually turning us into a well-disciplined peacetime unit, when it happened.

It sounded like an elephant stampede. I had never heard anything like it. At any moment I expected our cabin to be crushed. We ran outside. The enlisted men's barracks was on fire. Flames were being whipped around as if fanned by a hurricane. Men were jumping out the windows and running through the flames to safety. Inside, men rushed from their rooms into the hall only to run into each other. Ribs were cracked in the crunch. The barracks' long corridor, without a fire break, served as a chimney to suck the flames through the building, engulfing the entire structure in a matter of minutes. Miraculously those in the hall managed to get back in their rooms and out the windows before they were trapped. And miraculously no one was killed and none of the burns were serious. The most serious injuries were the broken ribs. And now the West Pointer had a blemish on his record, the equivalent of a Navy officer losing his ship on a reef.

Chapter 18

Sayonara

MY WIFE DOESN'T understand why we keep it. We know perfectly well where north is. We live on Lake Cayuga, a long, narrow body of water that runs from north to south, so all we have to do is look out the window for a point of reference. What I keep is a compass taken from a Japanese bomber at the air base in Kunsan that I mounted on the porch. It is my widow's walk. Along the coast of New England, 19th-century sea captains built a lookout on the roofs of their mansions from which their wives could scan the ocean for their return from a long voyage, a return that might never come — hence the name "widow's walk." Here in central New York State where I now live, miles from the ocean, many country homes have widow's walks vicariously sharing the drama of New England sea captains. But my compass isn't pointing north, it is pointing to the South Pacific, to the Yellow Sea, to the Philippines, to Korea, to memories.

It points to the the air base at Kunsan with its airplanes lined in row after row, not as warplanes ready in defense of Japan or to fly the ocean in search of a convoy to attack, but sitting there as the carrion of a dead war machine. And we were the vultures. I, in the navigator's seat of a bomber, with the aid of a hammer and a crowbar, removed my compass. A soldier climbed into the pilot's seat and began smashing the instrument panel with a hammer. It didn't matter, the plane was only going to rust away, but somehow it seemed like wanton destruction. I grabbed his arm and yelled, "What the hell are you doing?"

The startled soldier dropped his hammer and stammered, "Gee, Lieutenant, I didn't mean no harm. I'm making some toys out of bits and pieces of these old airplanes."

I felt stupid and told him to go ahead and get whatever he needed. Some men tore apart the planes for a reason, others ransacked them just for the hell of it. Either way, it didn't matter.

Japanese or American, so much that was once valued was no longer. Canned vegetable stew had long ago lost favor with our men once we were getting fresh meat. We had about 20 number ten cans of stew (restaurant size) that nobody would eat, which we gave to the Korean women who had been coming to the base to earn money doing our laundry. A few days later they were back, all smiles, with the empty cans; their way, we thought, of thanking us and asking for more. We had a few more cans, which we broke out to give them. Their smiles turned to a grimace. They pushed away the cans, shook their heads, and rubbed their stomachs, trying to tell us the stew didn't go down well. One of them giggled and pointed to her rear, making a face like she was in pain. One of our guys said, "I think she's trying to tell us it makes her ass sore and her shit burn."

"Please don't say shit," one of the men said, "you'll embarrass these ladies. Say feces."

The men started to laugh. The ladies giggled. They were enjoying the charade as much as we, but they had yet to get across what they had to say.

What did they want? The bold one who had pointed to her rear pointed to it again and frowned again, then pointed to the latrine and changed her frown to a smile. She held the can to simulate scooping up fecal matter. A light dawned on one of our men, "Holy crow, she wants to fill the cans with our . . ."

"Feces!" someone interjected.

The ladies went through a little act showing how they pour fecal matter on their gardens as fertilizer. Patting our stomachs and laughing, they said something that probably translated as, "Very strong food you eat, good fertilizer." We understood. Who needed translators? Once a week they came and gathered fertilizer for their gardens, saving us from a messy job. We dismissed these Koreans as simple people, but only now, years later, do we realize that they were way ahead of us in recycling.

By this time new men were coming into the outfit and older men were being sent home. All anyone could think of was home. Whenever someone got orders to leave, he would whoop and holler; then we would ask the lucky one, "How many points do you have?" The Army had established a point system of priorities for departure, points for winning a medal, points for participating in a campaign, and so on. I had points for two campaigns — one for Luzon, the other for Leyte, which was a joke. I did nothing there, just waited around in the main port of Tacloban for transportation north to Luzon. Off in the hills cleaning out pockets of Jap resistance, troops deserved points, but soldiers like me far from the fighting, lolling around in replacement depots, got just as many points. While I was there an enemy plane flew overhead causing some excitement, but hardly enough to qualify for campaign points. But deserved or not, I wasn't going to turn any down.

Length of service counted the most for points, and I had been in the Army longer than most with eight months into my fifth year of military service. Medals counted, and I had won a Bronze Star and a Combat Infantry Badge. Orders came for me to be aboard the USS *Golden City* scheduled to depart for Tacoma, Washington, on December 2, 1945. Arriving on December 12, I was shipped to Fort Knox, Kentucky, my last stop in the Army. I was placed on terminal leave, then left for Buffalo, my home town, arriving on December 31. On March 18, 1946, I was off the payroll. Officially, I was no longer a soldier.

The cavalcade was over.

Epilogue

I LEFT THE United States on a ship that passed under San Francisco's Golden Gate Bridge, not to see my country again until I entered the waters of Puget Sound on a ship bound for Tacoma. The glory of both sights was inspiring; both engendered wonder about my future. Although the future I had wondered about at San Francisco no longer held any secrets, Puget Sound marked the beginning of the rest of my life.

As we disembarked down the gangplank in Tacoma, some nice ladies, Red Cross volunteers I believe, welcomed us with a bottle of milk. Did I once like milk? It tasted funny. And the ladies were ugly — not that there was anything wrong with the shape of their torsos or legs, or their physiognomies; they certainly were pleasant. It was just that they were so ghastly pale. Were they sick? And they had painted their lips a bright red. Momentarily I wanted to return to Asia where the women's skin was a lovely shade and they didn't paint themselves to look like savages.

Good God, was this was my own, my native land? Was I going to fit in?

I was glad to run across Sergeant Kenneth Johnson, who, as it turned out, was also on his way home. Would that I could meet him again sometime, but I haven't seen or heard from him since that chance encounter. I hope all the things that had made him smile in Korea, when he reminisced about life back on the farm, were still in place when he got back home. No man deserved the good life more.

Tom Atchley and I have exchanged letters. He has led a good and quiet life, happily married in Arkansas. And Arndt Mueller stayed in the Army and was awarded the Distinguished Service Cross and the Distinguished Service Medal in Vietnam. He retired as a full colonel. For awhile I kept in touch with a few friends from my medical days, and a reunion of the 6th Infantry Division renewed a few Infantry friendships and developed a few more; but nothing could bring back the war years. When I was released from the service at Fort Knox, Kentucky, a curtain dropped on my Army life like the closing of a long-running play.

There was no applause when I got home. They hadn't seen the performance. My mother wanted me to wear civilian clothes as soon as possible; I wanted to strut around in my uniform. I had earned a Combat Infantry Badge and I wished to show it off. But most people didn't know what it signified, and if they did, few had any idea of what it took to earn one. The uniform was an anachronism. A new production had started. I bought civilian clothes to get in on the act.

One day in February of 1951, while hosting a group of industrialists at Cornell University where I was Director of Placement, I called a restaurant to make lunch reservations for my guests. With my head hunched over to hold the phone on my shoulder, I used my free hands to open my mail — another offer I couldn't refuse, a letter from the Army, calling me up for service in the Korean War. The curtain that I thought had dropped forever was being raised again.

Korea is cold in the winter; the terrain is rugged, and the population, I felt, resented our presence — ingredients that made it an especially miserable place to fight. Soldiers who fought there were never honored as they should have been. If I was going to die, I was determined to find a better way to do it than as an infantryman slogging through Korean mud. The Central Intelligence Agency, then located in the heart of Washington, D.C., offered me a better deal. I took it. Meanwhile, I flunked my Army physical; a problem left over from tropical diseases contracted in the Philippines got me off the hook.

I reported to the CIA, expecting to meet my new boss. Instead, the day began completing a long and involved questionnaire about my personal life. That finished, I was ushered into a small room where an attendant indicated I was to sit in chair that looked like something from a penitentiary, and made to seem the more so when wires from a machine were attached to my body. A dour interviewer said he wanted to go over my answers while I was hooked up to a lie detector. A question relating to homosexuality and another relating to communism gave me a twinge. The interviewer said nothing, droning on in a monotone to check my other answers. Apparently nothing registered on the polygraph. At the end of the questions, however, the interviewer said, "Now I want to go back to the question about homosexuality and communism." The day before, while having lunch in the State Department cafeteria, I unexpectedly ran across a college friend who I was pretty sure was homosexual. And one of my best friends was a radical, possibly a communist. At the time, Senator Joseph McCarthy was conducting a witch hunt to find and persecute radicals and suspected homosexuals, especially any he could find in the State Department. I told the interviewer I had a homosexual friend and a radical friend, then blurted, "But I'll be damned if I will give you their names." The interviewer, ever inscrutable, said nothing.

The next day I attended an orientation program for new employees conducted by Allen Dulles, then deputy director of the agency. What came through to me was an agency with two missions, each quite different: the first, to gather and analyze information of the kind that would help the President better understand the thinking and intentions of both our friends and foes around the world; the second, paramilitary, aimed at thwarting anything our foes might do to harm us. So it was that after the CIA analyzed the Vietnam problem, it recommended we not get involved. When, however, that advice was ignored and we did join the fray, the CIA jumped in with a paramilitary role.

The CIA had been looking for someone to call on various Eastern universities to find professors in various specialties who might be willing to serve as consultants. My job was to identify experts in a variety of fields who would be willing to consult for the agency, if needed. In addition, I helped recruit paramilitary personnel for a specialized mission. In a briefing with other recruiters assigned to the project, we were given highly classified information. The meeting completed and sworn to secrecy, we headed across the street to a small sandwich shop, sat down at a lunch counter, gave our orders for sandwiches that were then made right across the counter from us, and began talking in a normal voice about the *secret* mission. I completed my assignment with the CIA in six months and returned to Cornell, where I had been on leave.

Looking back to World War II, the train coming down from North Korea on that freezing winter's day stands out as my most memorable experience. I can still see people perched on the engine, on the roofs of the cars, and the cars actually bulging with passengers. I can still see old women clutching a few possessions, parents hanging on to their children, and the dead being pushed off the train. I can still see the family clinging to their baby, long frozen. Only mentally deranged leaders like Adolf Hitler and the Nazis would treat refugees like that. Yet here was evidence that the Soviet leaders and communists, too, were deranged. Subsequently, when hordes of Vietnamese were driven from the North to the South, I saw a repeat of communist atrocities.

When we got into the Vietnam war to put a stop to a type of government that fostered a system that would do that kind of thing, I was for joining the war. I was wrong.

My thinking was stuck in the past. Most thinking is stuck in the past. How we see things today is based on what we experienced yesterday. Carry-over thinking got us involved in Vietnam. And now the heritage of Vietnam, as well as that of Lebanon and the Sudan, has left us with carry-over thinking that is too readily applied to new and different situations. Witness Bosnia. Not that there aren't lessons to be learned from history, providing we understand the lessons. Ask "What's the good of history?" and you won't get much of an answer. We worry about the future, never considering that it is what happened in the past that created the forces that are propelling us today.

Cornell University hired me as its Placement Director on July 1, 1946.

I retired as the Director of the Cornell Career Center on July 1, 1984. I still go to the center now and then to counsel a student. At Cornell, over the years, I met many young people — black and white and diverse — who shared their hopes and ambitions with me. And unless the character of young men and women has drastically changed in the 11 years since I retired, the country will be in good hands in the 21st century. But I wouldn't trade their century for mine. Life hasn't always been easy, still the 20th century has to be one of the most remarkable in history. I am glad to have been a part of it.

Index